New Perspectives on Unemployment

edited by

Barbara A. P. Jones

Transaction Books
New Brunswick (USA) and London (UK)

Library of Congress Catalog Number: 83-24194
ISBN: 0-87855-978-7 (paper)
Printed in the United States of America

Library of Congress Cataloging in Publication Data
Main entry under title

New perspectives on unemployment.

   Papers presented at the Vivian Wilson Henderson lectures in labor eco-
nomics, held Oct. 28-Nov. 18, 1982, by the Southern Center for Studies in
Public Policy and the Dept. of Business Administration and Economics of
Clark College.

   1. Unemployed—United States—Addresses, essays, lectures. 2. Unemployment—United States—Addresses, essays, lectures. 3. Afro-Ameri-
cans—Employment—Addresses, essays, lectures. I. Jones, Barbara A.P.
II. Henderson, Vivian Wilson, d. 1976.
HD5724.N39 1984   331.13'7973   83-24194

ISBN: 0-87855-978-7 (pbk)

CONTENTS

Introduction

The Southern Center for Studies in Public Policy and the Department of Business Administration and Economics of Clark College presented the Vivian Wilson Henderson Lectures in Labor Economics, October 28 through November 18, 1982. The lecture series, "New Perspectives on Unemployment," was designed to provide new information and insight on what is indeed one of the most pressing problems facing the U.S. economy generally, and the black community in particular.

The lecture series featured outstanding economists with varying positions and proposed solutions to unemployment. The series opened with a critique of the prevailing theoretical framework used to analyze unemployment (i.e., neoclassical economic theory) and a discussion of an alternative to the paradigm by Professor David H. Swinton, director of the Southern Center for Studies in Public Policy and holder of the Clark College NEA Distinguished Professorship of Labor Economics.

The second lecture of the series by Professor Barry Bluestone of Boston College discussed the impact of the deindustrialization process on unemployment and prospects for the future. Professor Eleanor Holmes Norton, former chairman of the Equal Employment Opportunity Commission and professor of law at George Washington University, discussed affirmative action as a policy alternative for solving the problem of disproportionately high black unemployment.

The culminating event in the series was a symposium designed to present and compare diverse perspectives on the problem. The presentors were Professors Donald Harris of Stanford University, Nancy Barrett of American University, Glenn C. Loury of Harvard University, and Dr. Everson Hull, who is now deputy assistant secretary in the Office of

Policy, U.S. Department of Labor. The papers from this series (with the exception of Professor Norton's), together with a special tribute to the life and work of Vivian Wilson Henderson for whom the series was named, comprise this special publication. Also included is a paper by Joe T. Darden of Michigan State University, entitled "Racial Differences in Unemployment: A Spatial Perspective."

The Vivian Wilson Henderson lecture series, as well as this publication, are made possible by a grant through the United States Department of Labor, which established the National Economic Association Distinguished Professorship in Labor Economics Program at Clark College for 1982.

A Tribute to Vivian Wilson Henderson

The Vivian Wilson Henderson Lectures in Labor Economics were named for an outstanding labor economist, a scholar, teacher, college administrator, advisor to government, community leader, and activist. This series, "New Perspectives on Unemployment," which was designed to provide insights to scholars and to promote interest and understanding among the lay population, is consistent with the life and work of Dr. Henderson, which is discussed below.

When Dr. Henderson graduated from the University of Iowa in 1952, he became one of the first black Americans to earn a Ph.D. in economics. Early in his career he decided to pursue his professional activities through black colleges. His first teaching appointment in 1948 was at Prairie View A&M College. He moved to Fisk University in 1952 where he chaired the Department of Economics, established the Institute on Race Relations, and directed the summer school program. From Fisk, he went to Clark College in 1965 as president and remained there until his death in January 1976.

As an economist, his research interests were labor market experiences of black workers and the economic development of the South, but he also wrote on black colleges and the general status of the black population. He wrote *The Economic Status of Negroes* in 1963 and co-authored *The Advancing South: Manpower Prospects and Problems* in 1967. He contributed articles to a variety of periodicals, including the *Journal of Negro History, Daedalus,* and *Phylon.*

As an administrator, he was creative, an effective fund raiser, and adept at keeping his subordinates happy. Under his leadership, the Clark College curriculum expanded to provide new career-oriented options while the liberal arts tradition was maintained. The Southern Center for Studies in Public Policy was established and the college's total budget increased almost fivefold during his 10-year tenure.

Dr. Henderson's work was not confined to the college campus. He served in community organizations, such as the United Methodist Church, the National Urban League, NAACP, and the Martin Luther King Center for Social Change, and was appointed to numerous presidential task forces and commissions, such as the Commission on Rural Poverty under then President Lyndon B. Johnson. He was also a participant in the 1974 White House Conference on Inflation under President Gerald R. Ford. He sat on boards of major corporations, foundations, and research and educational institutions, including the Bendix Corporation, C&S Bank, the Ford Foundation, the National Bureau of Economic Research, Institute for Services to Education, the National Urban Coalition, the Voter Education Project, and American University.

Throughout his professional career, Dr. Henderson was an advocate for black institutions, particularly black colleges. He was instrumental in the organization of the Caucus of Black Economists, which was renamed the National Economic Association. He appeared before government councils and wrote articles explaining why black colleges should continue to exist. He was credited with having developed the strategy that saved Harlem's Freedom National Bank in 1975 when he put together a financial package that led to the bank's recapitalization.

In the 1960s, during the height of the civil rights movement, he left the classroom, the administrative offices, the corporate board rooms, and government chambers and took to the streets where he joined the student sit-in movement and masterminded a boycott of Nashville merchants. As two leading newspapers editorialized:

> He used his skills as an economist to bring about social change. He tried to show through the use of numbers how much discrimination cost the businesses of the region. He used numbers persuasively to show that desegregation and harmonious racial relations would help the towns and cities to grow . . . . There were many who sought to make that argument on emotional grounds, or moral grounds, but [he] managed to do it with numbers, and many who would have ignored less pragmatic entreaties were persuaded by his logic. (*Washington Post*, February 2, 1976)

> While some talked in terms of gross national product and disposable

income, Dr. Henderson talked about the need to evolve an economic strategy, a strategy that he saw as a marriage involving political, educational and social opportunities that could be developed into economic security for the poor. (*New York Times*, January 30, 1976)

Vernon Jordan, former president of the National Urban League, summed up his commitment to the civil rights movement when he said:

> Whenever the movement was going on and people needed documentation, you would find Viv, looking for ways to make the numbers say what people had been trying to say with their feet. . . . He was consumed with the civil rights movement and he was determined to make things right for black people. He did the research and walked the picket lines. No task was too small, no task was too big. (*Washington Post*, February 2, 1976)

For these reasons, this lecture series has been dedicated to the memory of Dr. Vivian Wilson Henderson, economist and president of Clark College, 1965-1976.

Barbara A.P. Jones

ORTHODOX AND SYSTEMIC EXPLANATIONS FOR UNEMPLOYMENT AND RACIAL INEQUALITY: IMPLICATIONS FOR POLICY

David H. Swinton

THE UNEMPLOYMENT PROBLEMS

In September 1982, after months of flirting with the 10% barrier, the unemployment rate reached 10.1%. This unemployment rate was the highest level of unemployment since the Great Depression. During the month of September more than 11 million Americans who were actively seeking work could not find jobs. Moreover, unemployment, which had been rising for over two years, showed no sign of abating in the short-term future. Projections by the Congressional Budget Office and others indicated that these high unemployment rates would persist through 1983. Moreover, trends in new filings for unemployment insurance suggested that the rate would rise to an even higher level in the short-term future.

The official unemployment statistics, however, only reveal a part of the serious labor market problems being experienced by American workers. The official rate of unemployment excludes a category called discouraged workers. These are individuals who have temporarily given up looking for jobs because they don't believe there are any jobs. These individuals would work if given the opportunity to work. According to the Bureau of Labor Statistics, an additional 1.6 million individuals were in the discouraged worker category during the month of September. The official unemployment rate does not account for people who have withdrawn from participation completely, and it takes no account of workers who were working part time because they are unable to find full-time jobs. During September another 5% of the work force fit into the latter category. Finally, the official rate does not account for the underemployed, those workers who are employed in marginal, low-wage jobs because they cannot find more remunerative employment. If these additional categories of workers were added to the officially unemployed we would have a picture of joblessness that is considerably more serious than is indicated by the official unemployment rate.

An official unemployment rate of 10.1%, indicating that one out of 10 Americans who would like to work and who is actually seeking work could not find a job, is already serious enough. However, there is another aspect of the employment situation that deserves special note. While the national unemployment rate for September was 10.1% and the unemployment rate for white Americans was 9%, 20.2% of the black labor force was unemployed, a postdepression record for Blacks. This percentage amounted to 2.3 million black individuals, one out of every five blacks that participated in the labor force. Black teenagers experienced a phenomenal unemployment rate of over 48%, roughly one out of every two black teenagers who was actively seeking employment. In addition to the high official unemployment in the black community, Blacks are disproportionately represented in each of the other categories noted above—discouraged workers, labor force dropouts, involuntary part-time workers, and underemployed.

Everybody recognizes that in the past few years we have experienced the worse recession in postwar history. However, periodic cyclical fluctuations have characterized our economy since records have been kept. In the usual course of things, good times are followed by bad times. Each period, each cycle, seems to follow the other in regular procession. Even in the so-called good times, millions of Americans remain unemployed and millions more remain underemployed. The existence of serious labor market problems for million of workers, therefore, is not unique to the recession but is a permanent feature of the American economy. This is especially true for the black population.

Moreover, the underlying problem of inequity hinted at in the statistics for black Americans is also a problem that persists through good times and bad. For example, in 1969, the lowest unemployment year experienced nationally since World War II, Blacks still experienced more than twice the unemployment rate of whites. More than 30% of black teenagers were unemployed and black males who worked earned on the average about two-thirds that of white males.

The point is that while the current serious situation calls our attention to these problems, unemployment problems have consistently been a part of the U.S. economic system. Unemployment is nothing new. Blacks have experienced few years in which they have had less than 10% unemployment. Over the last 28 years there were 18 years in which black unemployment was above 10%. Thus, the problem that has been dramatized by recent high levels of unemployment has existed throughout postwar U.S. economic history.

There are indications, however, that the current situation is more serious than previous postwar recessions. It seems to be the case that more than the usual periodic cyclical fluctuations may be involved in what is occurring now. It is clear that the basic industries have lost some of their competitive edge and fundamental industrial restructuring appears to be occurring in the United States. The current decline, therefore, may have secular as well as cyclical components, and the recovery will likely be slower than it has been in previous recessions. Fundamental economic changes may in fact be underway and something other than "business as usual" may be required to return to full employment. The issue, however, will not be discussed in this paper because of limitations of space and time.

TWO PERSPECTIVES ON UNEMPLOYMENT

At this point we will focus attention on the two undesirable facets of American economic experience discussed above: (1) the tendency for the economy to have a persistently high level of unemployment and to periodically experience cyclical fluctuations that create even more serious unemployment problems, and (2) the tendency of the economy to continuously concentrate excessively high relative levels of unemployment, underemployment, discouragement, and relatively low levels of wages within the black community. In recent years, these problems have been especially serious for black youth.

These are important problems. They have received a lot of attention from the general public, policymakers, and the media, and much energy has been devoted to efforts to understanding and finding solutions to them. Yet the problems persist. Why? In this essay I will explore the proposition that one of the major reasons so little headway has been made in solving these problems is that policies have been based on a faulty understanding of the problem, which has led to an emphasis on the wrong solutions.

The perspective that is guiding society's understanding, what I call throughout this essay the orthodox perspective, is wrong. This perspective, however, is the point of view of most researchers and policymakers. The prevailing orthodox view emphasizes the efficiency of a laissez faire market economy. In a laissez faire market economy, individuals determine their own actions. There is no control over their behavior by the government or any organized group. Each person is free to pursue whatever he/she thinks may be in his/her best interests. The orthodox theory assumes that this kind of system works well, produces a relatively full level of employment, and produces an equitable distribution of economic rewards and burdens. Liberal orthodoxy recognizes the need for minor nonsystemic intervention while conservative orthodoxy endorses complete laissez-faire.

The current and recent policies of the federal government flow out of this orthodox perspective. At the present time government policy is motivated by the conservative orthodox perspective, while for much of the previous two decades liberal orthodoxy had the ascendency. The conservative prescriptions primarily suggest the need to deregulate, to cease stifling individual initiatives, and to get the government out of the economy, then all will be well. The liberal prescriptions stress eliminating personal shortcomings of education, skills, or personality. The orthodox paradigm, whether liberal or conservative, emphasizes that the labor market problems that we observe are caused by the personal deficiencies of individual workers.

I argue, on the other hand, that these problems are in fact caused primarily by what I call systemic failures of the laissez faire system. By systemic failures I mean that the system fails to automatically create full employment and ensure equitable allocations of opportunities. Instead, there are flaws in the system that ensure that we have unemployment and inequitable distributions. These failures are seen as being endemic to the laissez faire system and specific policies are required to correct the difficulties. This proposition obviously stands in sharp contrast to what has been described as the prevailing view.

The primary purpose of this paper is to examine and critique the prevailing view. I will also present a few thoughts on the systemic perspective. It should be pointed out, however, that we are in the early stages of thinking about and applying this point of view to understanding economic problems. Therefore, I cannot present a fully developed systemic model of the economic system; however, I will be able to suggest how the systemic theory explains unemployment problems more effectively than the orthodox theory.

ORTHODOX EXPLANATIONS FOR THE EXISTENCE OF
UNEMPLOYMENT

The prevailing view, it seems, is that the economy may be studied, problems analyzed, and policy formulated as if the economy is best represented by what is known as a perfectly competitive economic model. The model makes specific assumptions about the way the world works, the amount of information people have, the ease with which people can make transactions, the extent to which resources can move from one sector to another, etc. Essentially, the perfectly competitive model assumes that there are no barriers to complete free flow of resources — nobody has any significant power or ability to influence economic outcomes, and all transactions are made frictionless. The model is an abstraction like all scientific models and is not intended to be an accurate depiction of reality. The key consideration is whether or not this abstraction reflects reality adequately enough to provide insight into labor market problems.

In the perfectly competitive world labor market, outcomes are the result of the atomistic decisions of millions of profit maximizing firms and tens of millions of satisfaction maximizing workers. Atomistic decisions mean that each individual economic agent makes decisions using his/her own judgment. There is no collusion, no rules, and no cartels. Each agent by himself/herself decides what he/she is going to do, how much labor he/she is going to sell, and how much labor he/she is going to buy. Each firm makes its decisions independent of what other firms may do. These models bring about efficient outcomes through the operation of what Adam Smith labeled the ''invisible hand.'' Allegedly this invisible hand working through markets brings about stable equilibrium outcomes, i.e., definitive predictable solutions that emerge from the atomistic interaction. By solutions I mean definite amounts of employment that each firm will offer, definite numbers of workers that each firm will hire, definite wages that each firm will pay, and definite amounts of labor that each worker will be willing to supply. Equilibrium means that all individuals and firms in the system are satisfied with the solution. They have no means or desire to change the outcomes. They are satisfied with what has been achieved given their resources and constraints. Such equilibria are supposedly automatically brought about by the invisible hand.

These equilibria are important in economic analysis because the equilibrium conditions have specific implications for employment and unemployment, and these implications are used to provide theoretical explanations for existing labor market problems. The solutions to this abstract model can be used by economists to predict what will happen in the real world only if the model in fact is a representation of the real world. Orthodox economists assume the usefulness of the model and explain events in the real world by applying the predictions of the model to real-world situations.

Although derivation of the results is beyond the scope of this essay, suffice it to say that the neoclassical theories lead to three important propositions that have provided the primary basis for orthodox empirical research and policy analysis on questions of unemployment and racial inequality in the labor market. The first proposition is that the demand for individual workers is determined primarily by their productivity (i.e., that an individual worker will be hired for as many hours and for as much money as is justified by that individual worker's ability to contribute to production). Usually productivity is measured by the skill of the individual, which in the human capital version of the theory is strongly influenced by the amount of training or education that the worker has. This theory thus provides a specific explanation of what determines labor market outcomes. Productivity is the primary determinant. Nothing else, neither luck, contacts, or prejudice, is assumed to exert a significant systematic influence on individual labor market success. The theory suggests that the wages, earnings, employment, unemployment, and occupation of an individual worker is systematically determined by this thing we call productivity.

The second proposition is that the amount of labor (i.e., the number of hours and the number of weeks that any given worker actually works) is determined by the worker's own choice of how to distribute his/her time between leisure and labor given the worker's productivity and market wages. It essentially concludes that any worker with the ability who wants to work can work as much as he/she wants so long as they are willing to work for the prevailing wages. The worker makes the choice. There are no barriers and sufficient opportunities are available.

The third proposition, and this is critical, is that the market or the invisible hand functions to ensure full employment of all labor that is willingly supplied at the prevailing wages, and to ensure the equalization of returns to all workers who are productively equivalent. Since the market does this automatically, neither the worker nor the government has to do it. The market forces take care of it, ensuring full employment and ensuring that workers who have equivalent productivity get the same wages, and the same number of hours. Thus, workers who are equally smart and equally motivated should end up with equal wages, equal hours of work, and equivalent occupations.

ORTHODOX EXPLANATION FOR UNEMPLOYMENT

These propositions have rather straight-forward implications for explaining the various problems identified above. Involuntary unemployment of people who want to work at the prevailing wage and are qualified to work is essentially ruled out. There is no way it can occur in this perfectly competitive model. If the world can be represented by the perfectly competitive model, then each worker can supply as much labor as desired at the prevailing wages appropriate for their productivity. The obvious implication is that there is a great deal of voluntarism in existing unemployment. The theory implies that people who are not working are not working either because they do not want to work or they are unwilling to work at the prevailing wages when a higher wage would be more than they are worth to the employer. The widely held view that the unemployed are simply the lazy and unrealistic thus seems to be a theoretical deduction from orthodox theory rather than an empirical proposition.

This is not a completely implausible explanation a priori. In fact, it likely applies to some people. There are some people who are not working because they do not want to work, and some people are not working because they are not willing to work for the prevailing wage. The question is whether this can explain the preponderance of the continuing high levels of unemployment, cyclical fluctuation in unemployment, or the racial differential in unemployment.

The only other explanation for high unemployment that seems consistent with the orthodox theory is the minimum wage. Minimum wages, which are set by government, can discourage employment even in an orthodox world. The argument is that since workers get paid wages equal to their marginal product, employers are only willing to hire workers so long as the wages they have to pay them are less than or equal to their marginal product. However, if employers are forced to pay a wage above the marginal product, the employer is not willing to hire the worker because paying such a wage will prevent the firm from making a profit. Therefore, establishing minimum wages in the orthodox world could prevent the employment of anyone whose productivity is lower than the minimum wage. This presumably provides an explanation consistent with orthodox theory for the unemployment of some workers who have low productivity; however, it offers no explanation consistent with the standard theory for why any high productivity worker is without a job.

Though the minimum wage has limited value in explaining persistent unemployment, its main value is in preserving orthodox theory because it permits orthodox theorists to maintain that the world really does work like the perfectly competitive model except for this outside government intervention, and if this government intervention would cease, the economy would operate as predicted by the perfectly competitive model with fewer problems than exist today. Thus, minimum wage theory eliminates the need to abandon the orthodox principles.

Orthodox theory provides no explanation for cyclical fluctuations in employment. Neither of the above two explanations of unemployment, the minimum wage or voluntarism, are capable of explaining why unemployment varies over time from 4% to 10%. It seems very unlikely that in one year 10% of the people are lazy and in a succeeding year 4% are so afflicted, or that such variation would occur on a regular basis. It also seems unlikely that the proportion of the workforce with too little producitivity to be hired in minimum wage jobs would vary from year to year. Thus, even orthodox theorists avoid these explanations in attempts to explain the business cycle. For the most part, business cycles are accepted as inevitable. Society has to live with them and ride them out.

ORTHODOX EXPLANATION FOR RACIAL INEQUALITY IN EMPLOYMENT

It is almost as easy to deduce explanations for racial inequality from orthodox theory. First the theory implies, as we stated, that equally productive workers have equal labor market outcomes. Therefore, in the standard orthodoxy, differences in black and white outcomes can only be explained if black workers are less productive than white workers. Blacks are assumed to have a lower distribution of marginal productivities than whites and correspondingly, therefore, to have lower distributions of market wages.

Gary Becker's modification of the standard orthodox theory allows the black wage rate to be lower than the white wage rate because of whites' dislike of association with blacks.[1] He calls this a taste for discrimination. This explanation is important because much of the difference in black/white wages cannot be explained by productivity differences. Although, on average, black workers have less education and other credentials than whites, empirical analyses have concluded that the productivity explanation does not provide an adequate explanation for observed racial differences in either employment or wages.[2]

To be consistent with standard orthodox theory, therefore, higher levels of black unemployment have to be attributed to one of two factors. According to the theory, everybody who is willing to work at the prevailing wage should be employed. Thus, so long as black workers are willing to work for wage rates that are justified by their productivity, having lower productivity than whites should have no impact on their level of employment. Blacks were fully employed during slavery. They were discriminated against but it did not keep them from being employed. How then can blacks be more unemployed than whites? There are two possible explanations. One, Blacks are less willing to work than whites, or two, the minimum wage. The former explanation says that Blacks are less willing to work for the prevailing wage attainable given their productivity. This is consistent with the standard notion of labor supply theory that the lower the wage the less labor is offered for sale. The argument is also sometimes made that black workers either are lazier or have unrealistic expectations. The other primary explanation combines the limited productivity argument with the impact of the minimum wage. If it is true that blacks are less productive, their natural wage rate would be less than the white wage rate. Thus, more Blacks would be below the level of productivity that would justify paying the minimum wage.[3]

IMPLICATIONS OF THE ORTHODOX THEORY

The prevailing theory gives the economic system a clean bill of health. Any maladjustments in the system are assumed to merely reflect temporary disequilibrium. Workers by and large get what they deserve in terms of employment and wages. If some workers are employed less than others it must be due to their limited productive capacity. The theory places the blame for unemployment problems on the personal characteristics of individuals and on government intervention. The same holds true for racial inequality. If Blacks have equal productivity they should have equal experiences. Thus, if they have unequal experiences it is primarily because they have unequal productivity.

The policy implications of this view are pretty straightforward. The relatively high level of unemployment would generally require little direct intervention into the labor market. Much of the unemployment may be voluntary, and there is no need to worry about that. Voluntary unemployment requires no corrective action; however, we might try to encourage people to work for the available wages or assist them in forming more reasonable wage expectations. These kinds of policies are consistent with orthodox theory. The cyclical component of unemployment will basically take care of itself. Some orthodox economists might advocate fiscal or monetary measures but that story is beyond the scope of this essay. No labor market policies are required.

Policy recommendations for dealing with the unemployment problems of low-skill workers would be to reduce the minimum wage and get rid of other government regulations that raise the cost of hiring workers. Liberal orthodoxy would advocate human capital development policies on the grounds that if you raise the productivity of these low-wage workers, their wages will rise. Increased productivity would make it profitable to employ them at or above the minimum wage. Proponents of this view recommend training programs for unemployed workers.

Several of these policies could be advocated to deal with racial inequality. The minimum wages could be reduced or eliminated to increase the number of low-productivity black workers employed, or human capital programs can be used to increase the productivity of those whose productivity does not justify paying them the minimum wage. Other orthodox theorists would advocate antidiscrimination programs to reduce the impact of the taste for discrimination. The prevailing view among orthodox theorists, however, is that discrimination is no longer a major barrier to black equality. This view which has emerged over the last 10 years[4] is based partly on the results of econometric investigations of black earnings ratios from the late 1960s to mid-1970s.

The gist of orthodox policy recommendations is to leave the system alone. To change the outcome, you have to change the individuals. The question is whether this orthodox view is correct and whether the policy prescriptions will work. A thorough critique of these views would take us too far afield; however, we shall sketch the argument concerning the shortcomings of the orthodox explanation.

INADEQUACY OF THE ORTHODOX VIEW

First, empirical work based on the orthodox theory has failed to establish its validity. The monthly Bureau of Labor Statistics surveys give ample testimony to the fact that there is considerable and persistent involuntary unemployment in our economy despite the prediction of its absence in the orthodox theory. In addition, studies have shown that the unemployed are generally willing to work for the same wages as workers with similar productivity.[5] In other words, when researchers have actually gone out and asked the unemployed whether they were looking for a job and what wage would they take to work in various types of jobs, they have found that the unemployed are generally willing to work at lower wages than the average wage currently prevailing in the various occupations. Since by definition one is voluntarily unemployed only if he/she is not willing to work at the prevailing wage, the empirical examination of the question of voluntary unemployment has not supported the orthodox conclusions that most unemployment is voluntary.

Moreover, empirical analyses of unemployment and earnings that relate earnings or unemployment to proxies for the productive characteristics of workers have repeatedly found that little of the variation of worker earnings can be accounted for by variations in their productive characteristics.[6] After reviewing much of this literature, Christopher Jencks in *Inequality* concluded that interpersonal differences and characteristics could not account for much of the existing inequality in our society. So although the orthodox theory hypothesizes that the differences are primarily due to productivity differences, when researchers go out and take measurements and test this hypothesis, they consistently find that the productivity factors cannot explain much of the racial differential. In other words, researchers consistently find that there are a lot of unemployed people who have the same apparent productivity characteristics as people who are employed. Frank Levy, in fact, in a recent analysis found that the unemployed were not very distinguishable from the employed in terms of their personal characteristics.[7] The employed were just as educated, just as experienced, had similar age distributions, and lived in the same places. They just happened to be unemployed. This does not seem unreasonable when we realize that by and large most people at all education levels, including high school dropouts, are employed. So it is obvious that there are many jobs in our economy that could be done by people with relatively low levels of education and skills.

A voluminous literature on the minimum wage has generally found that minimum wages have some employment impact but they have not found that the minimum wage is the major factor that accounts for persistent involuntary unemployment. Also, these studies have generally not found the minimum wage to be very significant[8] in explaining the disadvantages of lower skilled young black workers, the group for whom the minimum wage is supposed to have its greatest explanatory power.

Moreover, neoclassical policy prescriptions have not eliminated involuntary unemployment or racial inequality. Reliance on laissez faire throughout most of American history clearly did not eliminate either problem, and in the past several years since the government has drifted towards greater reliance on these policies the country has experienced a significant increase in unemployment and racial inequality.[9] It is important to keep in mind that it was not until relatively recent times that there has been any significant intervention in the labor market. Labor market intervention, as practiced today, began in the 1930s, and significant intervention, other than minimum wages and fair labor standards, has occurred only since the 1960s. If the laissez faire argument were valid, during the first 200-year history of the country there should have been full employment, equitable distributions, and low levels of racial inequality, but as we all know that certainly is not what we have observed.

There has been a steady upward drift in the education level of the work force in the last half century with a fairly sharp rise occurring in the last 20 years, particularly among Blacks. This rise has been motivated by the notion that education will increase one's chances for employment. Despite this increase in education and a significant narrowing of the differential between Blacks and whites, there has been no significant reduction in overall labor market inequality or in the level of involuntary unemployment. In fact, there has been a slight increase in earnings inequality and inequality in wage rates.[10] Some analysts suggest that a major consequence of this increase in educational attainment has been an increase in the number of overeducated workers.[11] Rumberger, following a recent analysis of the relationship between education and jobs, concludes that not only do we have a significant number of overeducated workers but the extent of overeducation increased during the 1970s, and black workers are more overeducated for their jobs than white workers. Blacks are already overeducated, yet orthodoxy suggests that Blacks are not being hired because they do not have enough education.

THE SYSTEMIC FAILURE HYPOTHESIS

Our analysis suggests that the basic theoretical explanation deduced from the orthodox theory is not verified empirically nor are the policy prescriptions very successful. We, therefore, are forced to the inescapable conclusion that the orthodox model does not provide an accurate, complete, or useful model of real world labor markets. Persistence of a phenomenon that a theory predicts should be absent suggests that there are flaws in the theory.[12] The orthodox model asserts the efficiency of the system by assumption, yet empirical evidence suggests that real-world labor market outcomes consistently violate two important conditions of efficiency. In particular, the labor market regularly fails to provide enough opportunities to fully employ all workers who are willing to work at the prevailing wages and the labor market persistently fails to bring about the condition in which workers of equivalent productivity achieve equal earnings and employment.

These results can only arise from systemic failure in the laissez faire system. In other words, these results can only arise if the economy does not operate like a perfectly competitive neoclassical model to automatically generate efficient and equitable distributions of employment opportunities. This is a profound conclusion pregnant with implications. If true, it implies that the economy needs help in achieving some of society's most valued social objectives. If help is not provided the country will continue to experience disappointment in regard to the level of employment, degree of poverty, and the degree of racial inequality.

While the invisible hand works reasonably well in the aggregate, most of the time the evidence suggests that it is incapable of providing either full employment, economic equity in general, or racial equality in particular. Obviously, the notion of the system's failure to achieve efficient outcomes is not new. John Maynard Keynes pointed this out in *The General Theory.*

Recently, the writings of the so-called segmented labor market theorists have also reflected the notion that the economy generates a structure of wages and earnings opportunities that has a built-in scarcity of good opportunities. The wage structure is also viewed as being relatively independent of the distribution of productive capacity among the available workforce. In other words, the segmented labor market theorists are saying that structural factors fix the structure of wages, employment opportunities, and occupations. These factors are independent of how many people we have with various skills.[13]

This notion is also implicit in the works of many of the institutional economists including Vivian Wilson Henderson. Some writers of the institutionalist school came to the conclusion that the notion of labor supply probably does not make any sense because workers essentially adapt to whatever structure of demand is out there.[14] Recent experience gives evidence in support of this notion. When the labor market first demanded computer programmers in large numbers in the 1960s, the workforce adapted. We now have approximately 500,000 people who are qualified to do computer programming. This illustrates that there is not usually any

problem of workers adopting to supply even highly technical skill requirements if in fact there is a demand for these skills.

The evidence seems to clearly indicate that the economic system rou-
tinely fails to provide either full employment or fair employment when
left to the operation of the invisible hand. The failure of the system to
achieve these outcomes is at the root of unemployment, underemployment, and the persistence of racial inequality. This systemic failure implies that at any given time there is a degree of inequality within the
economic system that is greater than the inequality that would be required by variation in the productive potential of individuals. Thus, some
individuals must by definition end up with lower economic rewards than
others who have equivalent productive potential. Some people must end
up making less than other people who are no different from them given
the structure of the economy.

The failure of the economic system to generate full employment of
resources on its own is a major systemic failure. This failure of the system means that some workers must be unemployed irrespective of the
adequacy of their productive potential. Many workers with qualifications
good enough to perform much of the work being done in our economy
will nonetheless be unemployed as long as the system works as it does.
The second major systemic failure is the inability of the market to provide
a structure of rewards or earnings opportunities that matches the distribution of potential productivity of available resources. As a consequence,
some workers will receive lower rewards than others with the same productive potential. A third major systemic failure is the failure of the economy to ensure equal access to human and other capital markets. This
failure means that some resources will not be able to develop their productive potential to the same extent as others with the same basic native
ability. All of these failures imply that the economy will be characterized
by both an inefficient and unequal distribution of employment and earnings. In essence the invisible hand will generally create a shortage of
opportunities relative to the productive potential of the available
workforce.

Even so, while a shortage of opportunities is a necessary condition for
the existence of racial inequities, it is not a sufficient condition. In a
nonracist world, the market institutions and processes that allocate opportunities to individuals would still operate so as to ensure an allocation of
available opportunities that is independent of race. Some individuals,
both Black and white, would receive lower outcomes than their produc-

tive potential warrants, but there would be no systematic disadvantage for Blacks.

However, the voluminous literature on racial differences that has continuously found large unexplained gaps in the labor market outcomes for Blacks and whites suggests that there are systematic disadvantages for Blacks. We therefore are forced to hypothesize that market institutions and processes that allocate opportunities operate to produce systematic racial biases in the allocation of available opportunities. Thus, the essential unfairness of the market allocation mechanism is a fourth systemic problem. This failure ensures that a disproportionate share of the inequality that results from the system's other failures is concentrated among the black population.

The systemic perspective provides a sharply different explanation for the existence of unemployment and racial inequality. First, it suggests that the high level of unemployment is due to the failure of the economy to generate enough jobs. This failure is seen to depend on factors other than the productive characteristics of workers. The excessive degree of racial inequality in the labor market is due to the inability of the economy to provide employment opportunities that match the productive potential of the workforce given the very complex institutional and social process that determines the wage structure. The important point here is that the productivity of workers is not the primary factor generating this wage structure or the overall structure of inequality. The high degree of racial inequality is due to systemic inequality and racial bias in institutions and labor market processes that control access to opportunities to gain human capital and credentials on the one hand and discrimination in labor market processes that determine access to job opportunities on the other hand.

This perspective clearly shifts the focus from the deficiencies of the individual worker to the deficiencies of the economic system. It suggests, contrary to the conclusion of the orthodox analysis, that most unemployed workers are sufficiently motivated and willing to work at available wages to be employed. Most low-wage workers have more than sufficient abilities and skills to perform adequately at much higher paying jobs; thus, their low wages are not due to their limited skills. Black workers, including black youth workers, have sufficient productive capacity, motivation, and skills to be fully employed if sufficient jobs were available. Black workers currently have sufficient productive potential to eliminate a large percentage of the earnings gaps if only they could receive equal opportunities to utilize this potential.[15]

The notion that systemic failures are at the root of our persistent labor market difficulties clearly has different policy implications. The perspective implies that policy should focus on alterations in the basic economic structure rather than "correcting" individual deficiencies. Laissez faire policies should not be expected to ensure the attainment of the social objectives of minimum unemployment and equitable opportunities for all. Given that the fundamental problems do not derive from inadequate education, training, or other human capital variables, training programs should not claim the highest level of attention. The perspective suggests that policies that directly increase the number of job slots would be the most effective approach to reducing unemployment. Policies that improve the structure of wages (i.e., increase the wages of low-wage jobs and increase the number of high-wage jobs) would be the most effective in reducing unwarranted inequality. Along with the above two types of policies, there is also a need for policies that reduce the systematic racial bias in the labor market institutions and processes that allocate job opportunities and opportunities for education and training.

NOTES

This paper was originally presented at the Vivian Wilson Henderson lectures, "Labor Economics," November 1982, at Clark College. I wish to express gratitude for the secretarial support provided by Ms. Danetta Matthews and Ms. Myra Murphy.

1. Gary Becker, *Economics of Discrimination*. 2nd ed. Chicago: University of Chicago Press, 1957, 1971.

2. See, e.g., Stanley Masters, *Black/White Income Differentials*. New York: Academic Press, Inc., 1975, and Christopher Jencks et al., *Inequality*. New York: Basic Books, Inc., 1972.

3. See David H. Swinton and Larry C. Morse, *The Source of Minority Youth Employment Problems*. Washington, D.C.: The Urban Institute, Research Paper, May 1983, for a discussion of the orthodox and alternative perspective.

4. See, e.g., James P. Smith and Finis Welch, *Race Differences In Earnings: A Survey and New Evidence*. Santa Monica: Rand, March 1978. Richard Freeman "Changes in the Labor Market of Black Americans 1948-1972," *Brookings Papers, 1973*.

5. See, e.g., Harvey R. Hamel, Melvin Goldberg, and Thomas W. Garnett, "Wage Expectations," in *Youth Unemployment and Minimum Wages,* Bulletin 1657 (Washington, DC: Bureau of Labor Statistics 1970), also Michael E. Borus, "Willingness to Work," in *Pathways to the Future: A Longitudinal Study of Young Americans,* by Michael E. Borus et al. Columbus, Ohio: Ohio State University Center for Human Resources Research, 1980. Both cited in Swinton and Morse, *The Source of Minority Youth Employment Problems,* Washington, D.C.: The Urban Institute, 1983.

6. See References cited in note 2 and also William Darity, Jr. "The Human Capital Approach to Black/White Income Inequality," *Journal of Human Resources,* Winter 1982. Robert Flanagan, "Discrimination Theory, Labor Turnover, and Racial Unemployment Differentials" *Journal of Human Resources,* vol. 13, no. 2, 1978. Harry Gilman, "Economic Discrimination and Unemployment." *Monthly Labor Review,* July

1975. Frank Levy "Have Black Men Gained In Employment?" *Brookings Papers on Economic Activity*, 2, 1980. Julianne Malveaux, *Unemployment Differentials by Race and Occupation.* Cambridge, Mass.: Unpublished Ph.D. dissertation, MIT, 1980. David H. Swinton "Dimensions and Causes of Youth Unemployment" in *Symposium on Minority Youth Employment Urban Disadvantaged Youth,* Washington, D.C.: Institute for Economic Development, 1980.

7. Frank Levy, "Have Black Men Gained in Employment." *Brookings Papers on Economic Activity,* 2, 1980.

8. See *Report of the Minimum Wage Study Commission, Vol. I.* Washington, D.C.: Minimum Wage Study Commission, 1981.

9. See David H. Swinton, "The Economic Status of the Black Population," *The State of Black America, 1983.* New York: The National Urban League, 1983.

10. See David H. Swinton, *Discrimination in Non-Competitive Labor Markets.* Cambridge, Mass.: Unpublished Ph.D. dissertation, Harvard University, 1975.

11. Ivar Berg, *Education and Jobs: The Great Training Robbery,* New York: Praeger, 1970, and Russell W. Rumberger, *Overeducation in the U.S. Labor Market,* New York: Praeger, 1981.

12. Kenneth J. Arrow, "Models of Job Discriminations," in A. J. Pascal, ed. *Racial Discrimination in Economic Life.* Lexington, Mass.: D.C. Heath, 1972.

13. See David Gordon, *Theories of Poverty and Unemployment,* Lexington: D.C. Heath and Company, 1972, Doeringer and Piore. "Unemployment and the Dual Labor Market." *The Public Interest,* no. 38, 1975. Barry Bluestone, *The Tripantite: Economy, Poverty and Human Resource Abstracts,* vol. 5, no. 4, July/August 1970.

14. See discussion in Swinton, *Discrimination in Non-Competitive Labor Markets,* chapter 3, for a review of some of the institutionalist notions and references to this literature.

15. David Swinton, *The Limits of Anti-Discrimination Policies,* Working Paper, Atlanta, Ga.: The Southern Center for Studies in Public Policy, 1982.

DEINDUSTRIALIZATION AND UNEMPLOYMENT IN AMERICA

Barry Bluestone

It is clear that we are living in strange times. Unemployment in September (1982) reached 10.1% with more than 11 million people out of work. Even Ronald Reagan tells us that unemployment will continue to rise until recovery sets in and then it will fall only very slowly. In most areas of the country, somewhere close to one in five non-whites are unemployed. Joblessness among youth exceeds 50% in many inner cities. Moreover, these statistics refer to the "survey week." Because workers are unemployed for a period of time, then go back to work, and other people become unemployed, the number of individuals who experience joblessness over the course of a year is much higher than even these statistics suggest. Over one-fifth of the labor force will experience unemployment sometime during this year. In round numbers that means somewhere between 24 and 26 million people.

Cities like Detroit, where I grew up, and Buffalo and St. Louis are on the verge of going out of business. Between 1970 and 1980, the City of St. Louis lost 27% of its population. Buffalo lost 23%; Detroit lost 19%. Detroit, with a population of almost two million in 1950, is down to less than 1.2 million today. We are abandoning communities throughout the country, and particularly in the industrial Midwest.

And yet, despite the highest unemployment in 40 years and the loss of some of our greatest cities, the stock market is on a bullish stampede. In October (1982) the Dow-Jones climbed more than 43 points in a single day — a record on the New York Stock Exchange. The exchange closed that day at 1000.65, the highest level in history. In London, in Australia, in Geneva, and in Tokyo, the stock markets recorded all-time highs. These are indeed strange times! Unemployment is at 10.1% and the stock market is going through the roof. Is the economy finally on the road to recovery? Is the Reagan program really working? Who are the real winners (and the real losers) in this game?

The economic issues we face today (e.g., unemployment, productivity decline, slow growth, the abandonment of community) are among the most difficult issues we have ever had to face. For somebody like me, who attended college in the 1960s and was a charter member of Students for a Democratic Society, the issues we fought over then were much easier than the ones that now must be faced. The issues in the 1960s concerned clear-cut fundamental human values. There was a definite right and wrong to the issues, and one hardly needed a sophisticated mathematical model to tell one from the other. There was, for example, no question at all about the sanctity of voting rights. In 1965, when friends and I drove down to Montgomery, Alabama, to march with Robert Moses of the Student Non-Violent Coordinating Committee and Martin Luther King, Jr., there was no question about what was right and what was wrong. There was no need to debate fine philosophical points or consult a computer before one could decide what needed to be done. For many of us, Vietnam was similar. There was a moral right and a moral wrong to that war and one did not need a Ph.D. to figure it out.

In the 1980s, the issues are extraordinarily more complex. I wish there were some simple analyses and simple solutions to unemployment, economic growth, the income distribution, and international economic equity, but there are none. The Kennedy tax cut, the development of the Great Society programs of Lyndon Johnson, and the War on Poverty all seemed to work during the 1960s. Unemployment plummeted to less than 4%, the incidence of poverty was cut nearly in half, and our standard of living increased dramatically. But in the 1970s these same programs failed to bring any additional improvement. Inflation soared, and along with high unemployment we learned about a new phenomenon: stagflation.

In 1980 the country turned to Reaganomics, a sharp departure from earlier policy. After two years of supply-side economics, it seems fair to call this experiment a substantial failure. Reaganomics never did make much sense theoretically: cutting taxes and boosting defense spending do not mix very well, creating massive deficits. Unfortunately at this point the Democrats have no alternative. The problems of unemployment, inflation, and falling incomes are indeed complex, and simple solutions simply will not do.

To begin to think about solutions, we need first to analyze what has been going on in the economy. My colleague, Bennett Harrison of MIT, and I have been trying to do this for a number of years. In 1980, the Progressive Alliance, a group of trade union, civil rights, environmental, women's rights, and antinuclear groups led by Douglas Fraser of the United Automobile Workers and Coretta Scott King, asked us to produce a "pamphlet" on the problem of plant closings. They requested that we assess the extent of the problem and the degree to which workers and communities suffered as the result of runaway shops and the permanent closing of factories, stores, and offices.

Ben and I took up the task. But because academics will be academics, our "pamphlet" took six months to complete, and when it was done it ran a total of 336 pages! It was hardly the kind of thing you could hand out at the factory gate. What prompted us to dig so deeply into the subject was our shock at finding how extensive was the problem and how devastating were its consequences.

To estimate the number of jobs affected by plant closings, we used data from the Dun & Bradstreet Corporation. Since the federal government collects practically no data on corporate investment and disinvestment, we were forced to rely on this private source. We had data only for 1969 through 1976, but using our computers we were able to answer a very important question: Of all the jobs that existed in the private sector in 1969, how many had disappeared as a result of plant (and store and office) closings by 1976? The number that came out of the computer was staggering. Between 1969 and 1976, 22.3 million jobs had disappeared as a result of plant closings (and the interstate and overseas movement of business establishments). This was equivalent to nearly 39% of all the jobs that had existed in 1969.

When we extrapolated these numbers to the entire decade of the 1970s, we concluded that somewhere between 32 and 38 million jobs had disappeared in this 10-year period. So staggering was the number that we ran the data through the computer several times before we were convinced we had not made a computational error.

There were other rather remarkable surprises in the data. Massive job loss in the Frost Belt — from the New England states through to the industrial Midwest — was expected, but we were hardly prepared for the results we found for the Sun Belt. It turns out that despite all of the hoopla about the booming South and Southwest, the number of jobs lost to plant closings during that 1969-76 period was nearly the same as disappeared in the deindustrialized North. The Sun Belt lost 11 million jobs while the Frost Belt lost 11.3. During that period over one million new jobs were created in Georgia by openings of new business establishments. But the state lost 587,000 jobs when plants closed down or moved away.

These extraordinary numbers reflect an amazing phenomenon. Among all business establishments existing in 1969, including the small "mom and pop" corner drugstore, the probability of being out of business by 1976 was greater than 50%. If we restrict the sample to include only manufacturing firms with 100 or more employees, the bankruptcy rate was still 30%. Only 7 out of 10 establishments in business in 1969 were still in business seven years later. Moreover, all of this occurred before, not after, the wave of plant closings later in the decade in basic industries such as auto, steel, and tires. What may be even more important is the fact that most of the large-scale closings occurred not because parent companies literally went out of business; in many cases, profitable establishments were closed down only because they were not profitable enough. Corporate managers decided they could increase earnings by closing down one set of operations and opening up another set somewhere else, often in a totally different business.

THE IMPACT OF PLANT CLOSINGS ON WORKERS AND THEIR COMMUNITIES

What is the impact of these closings? One way to answer this question is to analyze the earnings of those who lost their jobs. To do this we employed the Social Security Administration's Longitudinal Employer-Employee Data file (LEED), which contains information on 1% of all Social Security–covered workers for the years 1957-75. The data show quite convincingly that workers who lose their jobs permanently in such industries as auto and steel continue to be at an earnings disadvantage for years to come. After two years, the ex-autoworker makes 43% less than autoworkers who kept their jobs. Even after six years, the earnings loss is nearly 16%. Similar results are found for steelworkers, those in meat packing and aerospace, and even those who worked in lower-wage industries like men's clothing. The process of "creative destruction" that the famous Harvard economic historian, Joseph Schumpeter, wrote about in the 1940s is not bearing fruit. Workers are not being freed from lower-productivity, lower-wage jobs for work in higher-productivity, higher-wage jobs. The opposite is occurring. Workers are "skidding" downward in the occupational spectrum, not moving up to better jobs and a better standard of living.

The "high-tech" revolution is a case in point. High-technology jobs in the computer, medical instrument, and business systems industries are supposed to replace the jobs the country is losing in the old mill-based and smokestack industries. But do they? Using the LEED file again, we looked at New England's blossoming high-tech sector and asked, "What happened to all the workers who lost their jobs in the old mill-based industries in the region?" Did these workers find their way into high technology? The answer was a resounding no. Between 1957 and 1975, 833,000 workers were employed in the old mill-based industries (apparel, textiles, shoes, rubber goods, and the like) sometime during the period. By 1975, 674,000 no longer worked in those industries, largely because the firms had closed down. Some of the companies relocated in the South; some went to Singapore, South Korea, or Brazil. What happened to the workers? Of the 674,000 no longer in these industries, fewer than 3% were able to make the transition to the new high-tech sector. Five times as many (16%) skidded downard into retail trade and low-wage service jobs like those at K-Mart or McDonald's. Many left the labor force altogether, unable to find suitable employment. Others were forced to leave the region to search for jobs (often unsuccessfully) in other parts of the country. In short, the high-tech revolution, despite its great promise, has held out little hope for the victims of deindustrialization. As one displaced worker told a Boston TV newscaster, "My dream used to be to live better at age 50 than I am now at age 35. Now my dream is simply to survive."

THE OTHER COSTS OF UNEMPLOYMENT

The costs of unemployment go far beyond the loss of income. Professor Paula Rayman of Brandeis University and I recently completed a study of unemployed aircraft workers in Hartford, Connecticut. We interviewed over 200 workers, many of whom had worked at Pratt & Whitney, the nation's leading jet engine manufacturer. Workers told us that during their unemployment they suffered from chronic insomnia, headaches, and stomach ailments—all as a result of the personal and family tension associated with income insecurity. To cope with the financial drain of job loss, 36% of our sample depleted their entire savings. The first unexpected expense — caused by an illness or accident — placed some of these workers on the brink of bankruptcy. Three of the 80 workers who answered a detailed personal questionnaire reported they ultimately lost their homes to eviction or foreclosure. One worker I interviewed during the study told me that after 18 years in the plant he was given only a day's notice of layoff. Stunned, he picked up his tools and went home heart-sick. When his wife asked him what he had done to lose his job, he went beserk and beat her up. It was the first time in 20 years of marriage that he had ever laid a hand on her.

Other researchers have taken a broader look at the social consequences of unemployment. Dr. Harvey Brenner of Johns Hopkins University has statistically correlated a 1% increase in the aggregate unemployment rate sustained over a period of six years with:

- 37,000 total deaths.
- 920 suicides.
- 650 homicides.
- 500 deaths from cirrhosis of the liver.
- 4,000 admissions to state mental hospitals.
- 3,300 admissions to state prisons.

This is what unemployment does to workers and their families.

The impact on the community is also serious. In smaller towns where a single company dominates the local economy, a plant closing shrinks the community tax base. As a result, public services from police and fire protection to education and recreation suffer. In larger cities like Detroit, Buffalo, and St. Louis the loss of an entire industry like auto or steel often means the same thing. As a result, during the 1970s these three cities lost more than 20% of their population — the richer fleeing to the suburbs where better public services were maintained, the poorer to God-knows-where to seek any kind of job at all.

The impact on the national economy is also not to be underestimated. The Bureau of Economic Analysis of the U.S. Department of Commerce recently estimated that for every 1-point increase in the unemployment rate sustained over a year the nation loses $68 billion in output (gross national product) and $20 billion in tax revenues and must spend an additional $3.3 billion on unemployment benefits, public assistance, food stamps, and other programs to aid the jobless. If plant closings have been responsible for boosting the unemployment rate by just three points (out of the current 10.1%), then closings have accounted for nearly $200 billion — a fifth of a trillion! — in foregone output and contributed nearly $70 billion to the federal deficit.

Of course, the cost of plant closings and unemployment is not borne evenly across society. Greg Squires, who works for the United States Civil Rights Commission in Chicago, points out that black workers and their families are hurt disproportionately. Blacks are more concentrated in urban areas—particularly in the industrial Midwest, where the number of closings has been especially high—and Blacks are concentrated in those industries undergoing rapid deindustrialization — auto, steel, and tires. Moreover, plants are moving from central cities to suburban and rural areas where few Blacks currently live. In the years before Chrysler Corporation nearly went bankrupt, it was the largest employer of non-whites in the country. It was responsible for nearly 30% of all manufacturing jobs in Detroit. When the corporation shrank in size following reorganization, many Blacks were the victims. When a large chain of industrial laundries closed down in Detroit and moved to a rural community in Ohio, again the big losers were Black. Forty percent of the Detroit work force was Black; after relocation to rural Ohio, the company's black employment fell to 2%. This is surely part of the reason why black unemployment rates remain double the national average.

THE HISTORICAL ROOTS OF DEINDUSTRIALIZATION

Deindustrialization — a systematic decline in the industrial base — is happening to large chunks of America. It has had a more severe impact on the North than on the South, on Blacks more than on whites, but the entire nation is really the victim. Why have we all of a sudden lost our ability to thrive?

To understand deindustrialization requires that we trace American economic history from World War II. At the end of the war, the United States was the only major country left with its economy intact. Tremendous pent-up savings as a result of rationing during the war created the aggregate demand needed for a postwar spending spree at home. The signing of the Bretton Woods agreement in 1944 provided the basis for a new international economic order that gave the U.S. dollar reserve currency status worldwide. This helped to make the United States the largest exporter of goods and the largest investor of multinational capital. The combination of a domestic consumer-led boom at home and an open world market for our exports and investments was responsible for nearly two decades of unprecedented growth in the American economy — marred only temporarily by recessions in 1954, 1958, and 1961.

With the boom in economic growth came a boom in profits. American corporations were more profitable after World War II than at any time in history. By the early 1960s, it is estimated, the average rate of return on assets in the entire economy approached 16%. Stockholders were happy, and corporate managers were pleased with their own apparent performance.

Inevitably, in this context of buoyant profits, labor and the rest of the community came to demand their share of the rapidly expanding economic pie. What followed the war, then, was a heightened struggle over the terms of the "social contract" between labor and capital and over the extension of the government-provided "social wage" (or social safety net). Labor demanded higher wages, more fringe benefits, and greater input in the decisions over the speed and control of production. As one remarkable indication of the growth in the social contract, we can simply consider the physical size of negotiated labor-management agreements. The original collectively bargained agreement between the United Autoworkers Union (UAW) and General Motors (GM) was one-and-a-half pages in length — and was only because it was typed triple spaced, with large boldface type. Today's UAW-GM contract, including the master agreement plus local agreements, covers something like 14,000 pages and includes clauses on payment for every job, the pace of every machine, fringe benefits from holiday time to dental insurance, and conditions governing the subcontracting of work outside the GM system. Although they struggled against such an encroachment upon what they considered to be their prerogatives, businesses found that the new social contract was affordable, and in some sense, even productive. It provided a general level of labor peace that permitted continued economic growth and profitability.

This period also made affordable a veritable explosion in the social wage. Income transfers to the disadvantaged through unemployment benefits, workers' compensation, public assistance, social security, disability insurance, food stamps, and other programs mushroomed at both the state and federal level. Medicaid and Medicare were added to the federal government's responsibility to the poor and the elderly. And on top of these transfers came new government regulation: occupational health and safety rules, environmental legislation, equal opportunity laws, pension protection, and so on. The corporate sector fought these provisions, but learned (for the most part) to live with them and still make more than a tidy profit.

All of this changed rather dramatically near the end of the 1960s. International competition, which had hardly made a dent in American production since World War II, blossomed in the 1970s. The rebuilding of the European and Japanese economies was finally accomplished — in part through U.S. government support under the Marshall Plan and the generous granting of U.S. technology to foreign companies through licenses and joint ventures provided by American corporations. By the middle of the last decade, the rest of the developed world could easily compete with the United States in steel, autos, tires, petrochemicals, electronics, and even high technology.

Japan, of course, provides the best example. In 1960, the Japanese exported worldwide 38,809 motor vehicles. That is equivalent to the output from one single American auto assembly plant operating for no more than eight weeks with the usual two shifts. By 1980, Japan exported 2.3 million cars — to the United States alone — and six million vehicles worldwide. In building eleven million cars that year, they exceeded the total U.S. output by almost 20%. Moreover, the Japanese excelled in international trade across a broad range of goods. In 1979 Japan exported $26 billion worth of goods to the United States. The U.S., at best, could export $17.5 billion to them. Since that time the trade deficit has grown even larger.

But it is more than the total amount of imports and exports that is alarming. What Japan exports to us and what we export in return is the real shocker. Here is a list of the top six exports from Japan to America:

- Motor vehicles.
- Iron and steel plates.
- Truck and tractor chassis.
- Radios.
- Motorcycles and motorbikes.
- Audio and video tape recorders.

Here is the list of the leading exports from the U.S. to Japan:

- Soybeans.
- Corn.
- Fir logs.
- Hemlock logs.
- Coal.
- Wheat.
- Cotton.

It is only when we get to the eighth-most-important export — aircraft and aircraft engines — that one can find an American-manufactured product going to Japan. It is almost as though an underdeveloped country were trading its agricultural products for the high-tech products of a developed nation.

Japan became the leading world exporter during the 1970s, but Western Europe was not far behind. Moreover, the "Newly Industrialized Countries" (NIC's), including Taiwan, South Korea, Mexico, and Brazil, are now adding to the world's capacity to produce manufactured goods. The result: overcapacity in one key sector after another — steel, auto, electronics, and now perhaps even computers. The competition to sell one's products became fierce during the 1970s, putting tremendous pressure on prices. America's hegemony in the world market ended.

The impact on American corporate profits was severe. It is estimated that the average rate of return on all assets during the period 1963-66 was 15.5%. By 1967-70 the average profit rate had declined to 12.7%, and it continued to fall. In the following three years it was down to 10.1%, and finally from 1975 to 1978 it fell to 9.7%. The rise in international competition meant a rapid decline in profitability. In particular industries, the profit squeeze was even more dramatic. Profits in the auto industry fell by 65% between the early 1960s and the mid-1970s. In radios and TV, the decline was nearly 70%; in farm machinery, 51%; in electrical equipment, 49%; and in steel, 39%.

Now here is the crucial point. If you are a corporate manager and you see your profits eroding by a third or more — and your very job description reads "maximize profits" very much in the same way that the job of a major league batter is to maximize RBIs — what do you do? You have to find either a way to increase total revenues or some way to cut total costs.

Some firms attempted to boost revenues by introducing new products or new production processes or by reorganizing their work plans. But many more, it turns out, shifted their attention almost exclusively to finding ways of cutting costs — in particular, labor costs and their tax burdens. Ultimately it was precisely in the search for a cost-cutting strategy that management hit upon the tactic that resulted in the deindustrialization of America. The strategy they discovered was capital mobility. The way to cut labor costs, add flexibility to the production process, and reduce tax liability was simple: Move (or merely threaten to). Shifting capital from one corporate division to another was one tactic; disinvesting in one industry to invest in another was a second; moving from the North to the South was a third; moving from urban to rural areas was a fourth; and, of course, there was a rash of multinational activity with American corporations relocating domestic operations abroad.

Innovations in transportation and communications provided the "permissive technological environment'' that made the capital mobility strategy viable. The development of wide-body jet transports — the Boeing 747, the McDonnell-Douglas DC-10, and the Lockheed L-1011 — made it possible to move commodities, components, and executives at nearly the speed of sound. Pratt & Whitney, for example, the world's leader in aircraft engines, produces its F-100 military model in its East Hartford, Connecticut, plant. Half of the turbine rings for this engine are supplied by a small firm in South Glastonbury, Connecticut, only six miles away. The other half are imported from an equally small shop in Tel Aviv, Israel, nearly six thousand miles away. During the infamous February blizzard of '78, Pratt & Whitney found it easier to fly the Tel Aviv parts into its East Hartford plant (where it has an airport runway capable of landing the largest of the air transports) than to get parts by truck from its local supplier.

World sourcing of this type is more than a futuristic fairy tale; it is a present-day reality. The same is true in the auto industry, the computer industry, and in machine tools. My U.S.-assembled Volkswagon Rabbit has an engine from Brazil, wheels from Portugal, a radiator from Canada, a fuel injection system from West Germany, and an alternator and windshield from the United States. The "world" car, the "world" airplane, and the "world" computer terminal have been made possible by the permissive technological environment.

Satellite-linked computerized communications may be even more important to the capital mobility strategy. To take advantage of global production and global sourcing requires closely knit coordination of factory and sales activity. The new communications technology permits managers to be in immediate contact with each other and allows engineers to manage design and production tasks half a world away. It seemed like science fiction to me, but recently I was interviewed in Boston by an Australian correspondent in Sidney, Australia, and an economist in Melbourne. The communications link involved two satellites including Westar IV, four-dish antennae, and Lord knows how much electronics. Except for the one-second delay due to the enormous distances between us, the interviewers sounded as if they were in my living room. Normal telephone conversation is not as clear and static-free.

The ability to move things and people at nearly the speed of sound and information at nearly the speed of light makes the corporate environment markedly new. But even the opening of the Erie Canal in 1830 led to capital mobility. The canal ran 353 miles from Albany to Buffalo, New York — and at best one could move cargo along the route at 3.8 mph. But this was fast enough to lead to "runaway shops." Factories closed down in lower New York and opened up in new towns like Rochester, Syracuse, and Utica. Today, General Electric can close down a 60-year-old steam iron plant in Ontario, California, and expand operations at their plants in Singapore and Brazil. So it goes. If GE can make 16% rates of return on its South American investments and only 14% in the United States, one can bet that sooner or later the U.S. operation will be closed down — despite the fact that it is making a respectable profit in the old location.

THE OBJECT OF THE STRATEGY

What does the frenetic mobility of capital buy for American firms? The answer is the weakening or destruction of the old social contract and the old social wage. By moving or threatening to move, corporations are in perfect position to force one group of workers to compete directly with another. In such a climate of economic insecurity, the company can demand, and will often receive, major contract concessions. The so-called give-backs that have recently been granted by the auto and steel unions to their respective industries reflect not so much the current recession, but the longer-run threat of capital mobility. If the unions thought the jobs would come back as soon as the recession ended and production picked up, they would be extremely unlikely to grant such concessions. The capital mobility option is therefore the key.

Pratt & Whitney has used this strategy to destabilize the Machinist's Union in Connecticut. Instead of expanding one of their five plants in that state, they instead moved part of their production to a new facility located in the rural area around North Berwick, Maine, 200 miles away from their main assembly plant. The new nonunion plant produces the same parts as its unionized Southington, Connecticut, factory. Now when the union workers complain about working conditions, Pratt & Whitney simply threatens to move more production to Maine. In the process, the workers at both plants have lost almost all of their bargaining power. This "parallel production" strategy is analogous to the "multiple sourcing" ploy that the company forces on its parts suppliers — and it has the same effect: it empowers the powerful corporation and destabilizes the work force and the smaller companies that deal with it. What better way to lower one's costs and increase one's profit? The company obtains lower wages, fewer work rules, and generally less "uppity" workers, and from its suppliers, cheaper prices.

In the same way that corporations can use capital mobility to play one group of workers against another, it can force entire communities to compete for survival. By threatening to move, a corporation can "persuade" a community to offer it tax abatements and sometimes outright subsidies. Indeed, companies have become rather bold in their demands for a "good business climate." In 1976, the business community of Massachusetts was able to persuade the citizens of the state to vote down statewide referenda on a progressive income tax, a bottle bill, municipal-owned electric power, and utility rate regulation simply by running ads in the newspaper suggesting that such legislation would signal a "bad business climate" and therefore lead to job-destroying corporate disinvestment.

In the pursuit of the elusive "good business climate," states and local communities have fallen over each other offering ever greater sacrifices to the business community. The General Motors "Poletown" plant is a case in point. GM announced in 1980 that it was preparing to close down its last two production facilities permanently in the City of Detroit, but that it would be willing to build a brand-new Cadillac assembly plant in the city if the city were willing to make some concessions to the corporation. Otherwise the new plant would go to a southern location. What did GM demand of Coleman Young, the mayor of Detroit? First, the corporation wanted two-thirds of a square mile of land in the middle of the city. The area they wanted cleared was one of the most integrated in the city (51% white [Polish], 49% Black) where over 3,000 people lived. Mind you, this was not a "blighted area." Second, they wanted the city at taxpayer expense to relocate these 3,000 people, tear down and compensate 160 small businesses in the area, knock down a 170-bed hospital, remove three nursing homes, redirect two expressway on-off ramps, move a railroad right of way, and do something about the two-acre Jewish cemetery in the middle of the plot. The corporation wanted the city then to clear the land to a depth of 10 feet below grade so they would not have to worry about underground water, sewer, telephone, and gas lines. Finally, if the city agreed to all of this and then gave GM a 12-year 50% local tax abatement, the corporation would agree to build in Detroit. A conservative estimate of the cost to the city (including state and federal contributions) was $450 million dollars. What is interesting is that the City Council of Detroit, including its progressive and socialist members, voted unanimously to give into GM's outrageous demands. The people were removed by eminent domain; the houses, churches, businesses, nursing homes, and hospital were bull-dozed; and the plant has been built. Ironically, because of the depression in the auto industry, the plant is not occupied. Moreover, even if the plant were to go into full operation, only 6,200 jobs would be created — fully 600 less than the number eliminated by the closing of the other two GM facilties. Why did Detroit agree to such a lopsided deal? With unemployment approaching 20%, it really had no alternative.

Detroit is obviously not alone in its attempt to attract or retain industry. International Harvester notified Ft. Wayne, Indiana, and Springfield, Ohio, that it was going to close a plant in one of these two cities. By bidding to keep the jobs in their city, each community could determine which plant would be shut down. After much negotiation, Ft. Wayne offered the corporation $30 million in tax abatements, loan guarantees, and various subsidies to be paid by taxpayers. This should have won the day except for the fact that Springfield, Ohio offered $31 million. International Harvester will close the Ft. Wayne facility in April. Such poker games are now determining who becomes unemployed.

WHAT'S TO BE DONE?

The basic question we need to ask is the following: If the capital mobility option is being used to "discipline" labor and force communities to make concessions to business, how do we save communities from deindustrialization? What should be part of a progressive economic program?

Unfortunately there is no blueprint for economic survival. At best there is a loose bunch of economic ideas that need to be discussed and debated. First of all, we need to reconstruct the social wage. It is impossible to build a growing economy simply on the basis of fear. The Japanese have been able to develop an economy that is based on economic security (at least for a substantial portion of the labor force), and we should be able too. This means that we must reconstruct the unemployment benefit program, expand and improve — not gut — public assistance programs, and extend social legislation to cover plant closings. In particular we need to insist on prenotification of impending closings and on the providing of severance pay to workers according to seniority. Some 20 states have such bills pending in their legislatures and the Congress has considered, but not passed, the Ford-Riegel bill, which would accomplish this at the national level.

Legislation on plant closing will not stop capital from moving or solve the problem caused by the capital mobility option. But it will provide workers and communities with some time and resources to plan once a plant closing has been announced. With adequate notification it may be possible to save a plant, or at least find alternative employment for those whose jobs are threatened. Worker buyouts are another possibility that deserves attention.

We must caution, however, that rebuilding the social wage and extending it to plant closings is important medicine but no panacea. Such legislation is defensive in nature, defending workers against the vagaries of the economic system and the sometime dire certainties of management prerogatives. To truly rebuild the economy will take new progressive policies well beyond those provided by fiscal and monetary instruments.

A full employment federal tax and expenditure budget and an expansionary Federal Reserve Board strategy are sine qua nons for an economic renaissance, but these aggregate demand policies cannot deal effectively with the sectoral and regional specific dislocation occurring in the auto, steel, textile, and apparel industries or in cities like Detroit, Youngstown, and Buffalo, and in parts of the South. To smooth the transition from mill-based and smokestack industries to high-tech and services will require specific industrial policies that assist workers to acquire new skills and help communities acquire new jobs or retain ones they have.

With the success of Chrysler, we know it is possible to devise industrial policy instruments that can save part of the old manufacturing base and at least partially cushion the loss of jobs in particular communities. What we need to do is develop a national planning mechanism and a national development bank that can provide assistance to workers, industries, and communities not merely on an emergency ad hoc basis, but according to a carefully developed and reviewed plan. A new partnership between the private sector and government is needed.

The first step in generating such a plan must be taken at the local level, not at the top. Resources need to be made available to every community facing dislocation so that each can prepare redevelopment strategies. Such a strategy, including an assessment of community resources and community needs, has already been carried out for southeastern Michigan. The sophisticated methodology for creating this plan — including the use of occupation and industry data, demographic surveys, and "input-output" analysis — should be exported to other communities.

But this is only the start. We need to coordinate these plans at the federal level, assess what types of public "infrastructure" (from roads and bridges to health care facilities and new vocational education institutions) need to be constructed at all levels of government, and make sure that everyone affected by these plans has the opportunity to express an opinion. It is an ambitious agenda, but a necessary one.

The most important thing about the 1980s is that they have to be a decade of immense experimentation. Somewhat as in the 1930s, we must be willing to try out new ideas and pass new legislation. Knowing in advance that some of our experiments will fail, we must nonetheless not fear to try. In the 1980s we must bring together our concern for freedom and justice with our expertise for making the economy work better and more equitably. This is the struggle before us. It is extremely hard work, but I for one think we are up to it.

NOTE

This article was originally a speech sponsored by the Southern Center for Studies in Public Policy and delivered at Clark College in Atlanta, Georgia on November 4, 1982 as part of the Clark lecture series in honor of Vivian Wilson Henderson.

ECONOMICS, POLITICS, AND BLACKS

Glenn C. Loury

This article goes beyond the narrow confines of the subject black un-employment as usually conceived by economists to reflect upon the more general condition of Blacks in American society and what is to be done about it. Thus, this paper not only discusses the most recent statistics on minority unemployment and the mandate that they provide for change in the policies of the current administration, but takes a longer-term view of the prospects, economic and political, of the black population at this time. Those prospects are not very good, and the situation may soon become critical. It is imperative that a frank discussion of the factual nature of the black condition take place within the black community. For reasons I will detail below, that discussion does not seem to be taking place at present. Thus, an additional motive for broadening the topic somewhat is to get people talking about some subjects that have been taboo for far too long.

The black community in the United States is confronted with profound economic problems of which the current unemployment is only symptom-atic. These problems derive primarily from the fact that Blacks are the last of the many waves of migrants to have arrived in large numbers in American industrial centers earlier in this century and are only now com-ing to enjoy in comparable degree the possibilities of upward mobility that migration can afford.

Unfortunately, these possibilities are dwindling every day in the face of changes in the international economy that threaten the viability of impor-tant segments of American industry. Shrinking markets at home and abroad threaten many hundreds of thousands of blue-collar workers in basic industries like autos, steel, rubber, and glass with loss of their jobs, or at best with loss of some wage and fringe benefits to which they have come to feel entitled. The world economy is in a period of fundamental transition. The dominance of United States firms in world markets stemming from the post–World War II arrangement came to an end over a decade ago. We now face vigorous competition from the Japanese and West Europeans in a host of areas where we were formerly dominant, including some high-technology pursuits.

Emerging economies, such as those of South Korea, Taiwan, Brazil, and Mexico, will in a few years begin to mount their own challenges to our relatively privileged economic position. These countries represent a potential industrial work force of many hundreds of millions. Once equipped with capital and basic skills, as they are rapidly coming to be, they will encounter few barriers to their effective competition with American workers for the privilege of manufacturing the world's industrial and consumer goods.

The United States will be forced continually to modernize, introduce new products and technologies, reduce costs, and find better ways of serving the world's markets, or else see its workers' living standard eroded through foreign wage competition or domestic unemployment, or both. Thus, in the future American workers will not be able to rely on the following in their parents' footsteps to prosperity via stable high-paying employment in the array of currently existing industries. To maintain our status will require constant advance in technology and an ever increasing sophistication of the American worker.

It remains to be seen whether our economy will be able to meet the challenges posed by growing foreign competition in the coming decades. But it is clear that, even if successful, some of us will be better able to avail ourselves of the opportunities than others. An 18-year-old black youth entering the labor force today will retire in the year 2030. No one can say what the world economic landscape will look like at that time. The only certainty is that it will be quite different from what it is today. To participate fully in the economic success Americans as a whole will, one hopes, attain over the coming decades, that young person must be in possession of basic skills sufficient to permit him or her to adapt to the inevitably changing requirements of the marketplace.

Many of our young people—too many—are not being equipped with those basic skills. This fact is evidenced by the recently announced disparity between black and white children on the College Board's SAT examination. The mean mathematics score for Blacks was 121 points lower than that for whites; there were 200 whites for every Black scoring above 750, and 100 whites for every Black above 650.[1] The problem of poor inner-city schools is too well known to require elaboration here. Suffice it to say that an 18-year-old who begins adult life without the ability to do simple mathematics or use the language tolerably well is at an enormous disadvantage relative to his or her better-prepared peers. That teenager is likely to end up in a losing competition with much cheaper semiskilled labor elsewhere in the world. As the American economy adjusts to competitive pressures and changing technology, the American worker will be adjusting as well. Those workers hampered by second-rate education will find it quite difficult to manage these changes.

Associated with these economic difficulties, which I see as becoming even more pronounced in the years ahead, is a changing political environment that Blacks must confront. It is apparent that the era of big-spending, liberal, interventionist public policy, in which Washington takes the lead in confronting the problems of lower-class people, has passed on, perhaps never to return. Neoliberalism is the order of the day among "progressive" Democrats who want to be elected to national office.

As far as I can make out, this seems to mean adopting realistic policies that avoid the excesses of the Great Society without abandoning compassion for the underdog. Where the inner-city black poor fit into this scheme is something that liberal politicians have not been so forthcoming about. The budget reductions of the Reagan administration, which were agreed to, however reluctantly, by the Congress, fell heavily upon this relatively voiceless constituency. A study by the Urban Institute of the impact of enacted budget reductions during the first year of the new administration revealed that the burden of cuts was relatively greatest in those programs serving primarily the poorest families. Projected savings through fiscal year 1984 as a percentage of 1981 outlays was 0.8% for income security for veterans but 34.5% for low-income energy assistance; 1.6% for federal employee retirement and disability, but 16.3% for Aid to Families with Dependent Children (AFDC): 1.6% for Social Security, but 18.6% for food stamps.[2]

Talk of reducing the costs associated with agricultural price supports was derided by many Democrats as improper given the recession in agriculture today, though those same representatives in many cases found no problem in voting for a reduction of more than 60% in federal expenditures on employment and training between fiscal years 1981 and 1983. The Democratic response to the president's most recent State of the Union address was a highly polished film with voice-over, depicting the many needy Americans who were being forgotten by the Republicans but remembered by the Democrats. Yet, nowhere among the film's elderly and indigent unemployed voters who would be helped by returning the Democrats to power was there to be found a black welfare mother with four hungry children to feed and no husband or job. In short, the image of those whom the Democrats would help did not include any representatives of the group in our society arguably most in need of assistance. One can only conclude that the political liability of including such people in the demographic statement outweighed whatever benefits would be derived therefrom.

The point I am trying to make is that the country is moving to the right politically. Poor Blacks are no longer "in," and may in fact have become a political liability for those who exhibit too much conern for their welfare. Many observers were quick to point out how the election of 1976 was won for Carter by the black vote, which was overwhelmingly Democratic. Fewer have noted that the election of 1980 was won for the Republicans by the blue-collar vote, which defected from Democratic ranks in such large numbers that Lane Kirkland of the AFL-CIO did not dare to endorse a candidate. In one industrial state after another, Reagan gained victory on the backs of white working-class voters disaffected with Carter's version of liberalism.

This phenomenon should not be overlooked by black politicians. Blacks can no longer rely on their traditional allies in the Democratic party to enact transfers from an increasingly hostile public to their community. It is quite clear that the civil rights issues have become secondary on the political agendas of the powerful, and that many voters are more concerned about their own security than about solving the intractable problems of ghetto poverty.

Thus, the situation of many in the black community is fraught with danger. In what Lester Thurow has termed the "zero-sum society,"[3] competing claimants—the elderly, the farmers, unionized workers in declining sectors, businessmen seeking protection from foreign competition—all struggle through the political system along with the black poor for attention from government to their problems. The political agenda is crowded with claims of these varied groups, and not all of them can be served. As the memory of the moral outrage of racism which many on the left in American politics fought against in the 1950s and 1960s fades, it becomes less than obvious that the concerns of ghetto-dwelling low-income Blacks will maintain a prominent place on the liberal agenda. It therefore becomes imperative that persons in the black community with positions of influence begin to examine alternative avenues of political advocacy that address the most serious problems of the community, recognizing that help from liberals may not be forthcoming.

The formulation of such an alternative advocacy requires an objective examination of the resources that are at their disposal and the conditions that inhibit our advance. Neither of these subjects has been adequately discussed by black leaders and intellectuals. There has been a tendency to understate the internal capacities of the black community by denying the quite significant expansion of opportunities for Blacks that has occurred in the past two decades. There has also been a proclivity to ignore the extent to which difficulties in the community derive from patterns of behavior among Blacks that are destructive of the social fiber and that are within the community's ability to control. I believe that this unwillingness (or inability) to acknowledge these internal assets and liabilities fully, and to act on the implications of such acknowledgment, constitutes a major threat to the long-term viability of the group. Below is a discussion in more detail of the nature of this problem and some of its possible causes.

There has been a dramatic change in the structure of opportunities facing Blacks in the last 20 years. The systematic exclusion from the institutions of power and influence that characterized the first 100 years after emancipation has been significantly eroded as a consequence of civil rights enforcement, changes in the hiring practices of large corporations, and the admissions policies of elite universities and professional schools. The relative number of Blacks studying law, medicine, and business administration has increased markedly during this period. Earnings differences among employed, well-educated Blacks and whites have dwindled, as reflected by the fact that black male college graduates averaged weekly earnings at 88% of the comparable level for whites in 1978, in contrast to a 62% figure in 1967. Among the youngest workers with college diplomas, Blacks averaged an annual income that was 98% of the white average in 1978, in contrast to a 74% figure in 1967.[4] (This was for workers with five years or less of labor market experience.)

There has been established in the last decade a sizable enforcement apparatus for dealing with violations of the civil rights statutes and executive orders. Both the budget and the number of cases resolved of the Equal Employment Opportunity Commission (EEOC) grew by a factor of 10 during the 1970s. In 1979 civil rights cases constituted over 20% of all cases tried in the federal courts. The activities of the Office of Federal Contract Compliance, which enforces affirmative action standards that federal contractors must meet, also expanded dramatically during this decade. Now, all of this antidiscrimination enforcement activity does not, of course, mean that racial discrimination has come to an end—indeed, one might take the increase in lawsuits as evidence of a worsening problem of discrimination. What is undeniable however, is that there is in place an institutionalized mechanism of redress that has significantly increased the risk to employers of overt racial discrimination and that has grown in importance during the same period in which the earnings disparity between comparably placed Blacks and whites has been diminished to historically unprecedented levels.

Yet not all Blacks have shared equally in the gains made possible by this structural change. Income inequality within the black community has increased in the last decade and by some measures is actually greater than inequality among whites. In 1977 the wealthiest 20% of black families earned 44.9% of all income accruing to Blacks, while the top 20% of white families received 41.5% of white income. The unemployment problems of inner-city black young people have been widely cited. These numbers are often used to document the generally poor state of black people in the currently depressed economy, but really reflect the especially grave circumstance affecting the poorest black families.

While the relative earnings of college-educated young Blacks were increasing during the 1970s the comparable situation of Blacks with less than a high school diploma was actually deteriorating. The average black worker with five years or less of labor market experience and 8-11 years of schooling earned 79% as much as a similar white in 1967, but only 69% of a comparable white worker's income in 1978.

The fraction of children in the black community who live below the poverty line has continued to grow throughout this period, until today more than two in five black children are in this circumstance.[5] In certain central city areas— Chicago, Detroit, Philadelphia, Newark, Oakland, Los Angeles, St. Louis, New York— the fraction ranges from one-half to two-thirds. These children are concentrated in single-parent families, are often dependent on state and federal aid for their economic support, are more likely to live in public housing than the rest of the black population, and are subject to the negative influences of high crime rates in their communities and poor-quality public education. This current cohort of young Blacks, roughly 40% of the black youth, poses the most serious and intractable problem to concerned observers of the black community. Their prospects for finding a self-supporting role in the changing economic environment of the coming decades seem dim.

Thus, there has been developing in the past 10 years or so a schism in the economic prospects of black Americans. Opportunity for participation in the mainstream of corporate, academic, and government life has increased markedly in this period, while the fraction of the community unlikely to be in a position to make use of the new opportunities has been growing. This is hardly a novel thesis; it has been raised by several commentators in the past decade. Most recently, William Wilson, in his book *The Declining Significance of Race*,[6] has pointed to the worsening position of the black underclass and argued that its problems are quite different from those facing the rest of the black population.

This observation of widening differences among Blacks has been fiercely resisted by many in the black community. Numerous tracts have been written "proving" that things have been getting worse for Blacks as a whole, denouncing the "myth of black progress," showing that talk of an emerging black middle class is premature, and insisting that the role of racism as the fundamental cause of the problems of Blacks has not diminished. The concept conveyed by such argument is that there is an undifferentiated racial experience in American society, which all Blacks endure though some are less damaged than others by it, and which people of good will must continue to oppose through the support of civil rights advocacy as traditionally conceived. This position is reflected in the following comments of black psychologist Kenneth Clark:

> American racism was and remains "democratic" in that all Blacks were perceived and treated alike. American Whites tended to react to a person of color as if he were automatically lower class. This was and continues to be generally true without regard to distinctions among individual Blacks in terms of education, economic status, and other generally accepted class symbols.[7]

I believe this to be a seriously anachronistic reading of the current condition of black Americans. Its acceptance obviates the raising of certain questions central to the dilemma of Blacks today. What, for example, should be the responsibility of the black middle class in alleviating the conditions of poor Blacks, especially given the reduced involvement of the federal government? To what extent is the current program of the civil rights community likely to have a beneficial impact on the conditions of the ghetto-dwelling underclass? What role do internal conditions and behaviors within the low-income black population—conditions and behaviors that middle-class Blacks themselves strive to avoid— play in perpetuating the impoverished circumstances of these communities? How, if at all, can a genuine sense of nationalism and unity be forged among Blacks, given the great disparity in our material condition?

These are perennial questions that have today assumed special urgency. Fifteen years ago Martin Luther King wrote:

> It is time for the Negro haves to join hands with the Negro have-nots and, with compassion, journey into that other country of hurt and denial. It is time for the Negro middle class to rise up from its stool of indifference, to retreat from its flight into unreality and to bring its full resources— its heart, its mind and its checkbook— to the aid of the less fortunate brother.[8]

Those words ring true today, and the capacity to render such assistance is vastly greater than it was in 1967. Yet there is virtual silence from our intellectual leadership regarding how this gap might be bridged, a silence encouraged by those who assert that the gap does not exist.

The existence of this disparity is attested not only by the advance in economic opportunity for skilled black workers, but also by the wretched and deteriorating conditions of social life in inner-city black communities. Here too there has been a tendency to either deny or ignore the evolving factual circumstance. In the 1960s it became popular among black intellectuals to dismiss characterizations of the low-income black population as pathological or deviant, on the grounds that such conceptions placed blame upon the victim of oppression. The view was widely propounded that criminal violence within the ghetto, or the growing incidence of illegitimacy and single parenthood were but the obvious consequences of racial oppression and would diminish as that oppression was overcome.[9]

These phenomena have become even more pronounced over the past two decades and, in my judgment, now pose a serious obstacle to improvement of the condition of the ghetto poor. According to the 1980 U.S. Census, 42.2% of black children under 18 years old lived with both parents, in contrast to 82.7% of whites. (Indeed, 11.5% of young black people lived with neither parent! The comparable number for whites was 2%). To get some idea of the nature of the change underway among Blacks, it is worth noting that in 1970 nearly 60% of children were living in homes with both parents present. In 1970 30.6% of the black families with children present were headed by women; by 1979 the proportion was 45.6%.

I am not arguing that there is something wrong with women heading households, or something intrinsically virtuous about the conventional two-parent arrangement. But I do assert that the economic opportunities of children raised in homes with both parents present are superior to those in which the mother struggles to raise her children alone. The median family income of female-headed households is roughly 54% of that attained by all families, and the median female-headed black family earns about three-fifths of the income of a comparable female-headed white home. Thus, children growing up in families headed by black women are the poorest young people in American society.

In 1978 41.2% of black children lived in families below the poverty line, compared to a mere 11% of whites. Although it is clear to me that this difference partly reflects a divergence in economic opportunity between racial groups, it seems undeniable that it also reflects the above-cited divergence in behavior between the communities. Moreover, the pattern seems to be emerging as a fixture in Afro-American life. In 1978 there were 83.9 out-of-wedlock births for every 1,000 black women between the ages of 15 and 19; the rate for white teenagers was less than one-sixth as great. What chance will a 16-year-old black mother and her baby have in the American economy of the future?

As profound as these developments are for the social character of the black community, and as alarming as the implications of these trends are for the future economic prospects of today's black youth, there seems to be a deafening silence from our intellectual leadership regarding how this problem is to be dealt with. It has been left to feminist black writers such as Ntozake Shange, Alice Walker, and Michelle Wallace to give voice to the frustration and rage that lurk beneath the surface.

Nearly 20 years ago, in the infamous Moynihan Report, attention was called to these developments within the black family. That flawed study was widely ridiculed by black sociologists, not without reason. But the basic trend to which it called attention may, in retrospect, be seen as having been maintained. The magnitude of the problem when Moynihan wrote was half what it is today. Must we wait another 20 years before this phenomenon is regarded with the urgency it merits? Or are we to suppose that this is yet another manifestation of racism that will be resolved when white America owns up to its moral responsibilities? And, what if it never does? Clearly, the pattern of early unwed pregnancy in our community has something to do with values, as well as with economic opportunities. Equally clearly, these are values not shared by the black middle class, whose members would be appalled at the prospect of their daughters with an AFDC-supported baby at age 18. Why are they silent?

Criminal behavior is another area of concern that has been poorly handled by black intellectual leadership. To be sure, inner-city crime is associated with the scarcity of jobs for young men in these communities. But the nature and extent of criminal behavior among ghetto-dwelling young black men cannot, I suggest, be so easily rationalized. The fact is that Blacks are nearly six times as likely as whites to be victims of homicide. The elderly Black living in an urban area is more than twice as likely as an elderly white to be a victim of a personal crime of violence. In 1980 a Black was nearly 10 times as likely as a white to be charged with murder, more than 10 times as likely to be charged with forcible rape, and more than 15 times as likely to be charged with robbery.[10]

Blacks today represent approximately 49% of the incarcerated population in the United States. We can account for some of this disparity in the crime statistics by reference to a lack of impartiality in the administration of criminal justice and can rationalize some as the behavior of economically desperate men trying to feed their families. But how many of us really find those adequate explanations? Surely, the vast majority of inner-city black residents who eschew this option, but are all too often the victims of its exercise by others, can take little comfort in our rationalizations. Nobody concerned about the welfare of black people can condone or overlook the effects of this behavior on their communities. Surely there is a way for black intellectuals to come out in opposition to this mode of behavior without betraying group loyalties. Talk of incarcerated felons as noble rebels against the system, as political prisoners worthy of our pity or respect, or both, is sheer lunacy in this environment. Would not a healthier response from the black community be to make its opposition to this behavior by a small minority of its young men known, to express unambiguously its values and its outrage? Why has such a response not been forthcoming?

I will not claim here to have found answers to all of the vexing questions I have raised in this paper. But I do want to suggest some considerations that play a role in perpetuating this intellectual dilemma. Foremost among these is the concern that frank discussion among Blacks of our own faults and failings will lend aid and comfort to political enemies— racists who would prove the innate inferiority of Blacks. We have been unwilling to talk about the culpability of our own, when it has been appropriate, for fear that others would use this talk as excuse to abandon the black poor, or as reason to damn them.

We have on the whole accepted uncritically a "systemic" explanation of failures in our community, attributing these problems primarily to failures of American society in general and thus absolving the individuals whose behavior is at issue. As a result, we have taught a generation of Blacks to look without, not within, for the source of alleviation of their suffering. And in doing so, we have helped to make this generation more dependent on the largess and liberalism of the American majority and less capable of surviving the kind of hostility our forebears nobly withstood. For, by failing to instill in our young people a sense of responsibility for their personal conduct, we risk removing the single most important tool for change in their circumstance—namely, a belief in themselves. We make of them instead a permanent class of special pleaders, prostrate before the American polity. This is a formula for disaster.

In the work cited earlier, Martin Luther King said:

> It is not a sign of weakness, but a sign of high maturity, to rise to the level of self-criticism. Through group unity we must convey to one another that our women must be respected, and that life is too precious to be destroyed in a Saturday night brawl, or a gang execution. Through community agencies and religious institutions we must develop a positive program through which Negro youth can become adjusted to urban living and improve their general level of behavior.[11]

I think those were wise words, indeed. One might advance the notion that the Black Power–Black Pride movement wrought a revolution in self-perception among Blacks that remains seriously incomplete. We came to accept widely the teachings of this movement to the effect that is all right not to have light skin or ''good'' hair, that there is much to be proud of in the history and culture of black people, and that continual reference to the judgment of whites as a benchmark for the Blacks' self-esteem was to be avoided. Yet, we somehow seem not to have taken these teachings fully to heart. To be unable to appraise critically, and accept responsibility for, one's own failings, owing to fear that the negative views of others will be supported, is to show a lack of maturity and self-confidence. Arguably, the most valuable asset of any community of mutually concerned individuals is their ability to exchange criticism without undermining the basis of their cooperative association. This is an asset of which the black community is in short supply.

Thus, I am convinced that black intellectuals have much unfinished business to attend. Formulating a conception of our collective identity that can serve as the basis for building genuine communal association reaching across class lines should be near the top of the list of things to do. The relatively affluent members of the black community have, I believe, a responsibility to address themselves in a substantive, resourceful, time-consuming way to the plight of the underclass. Their use of race must be transformed beyond the self-serving claims for special favor grounded on the suffering of the poor Blacks, which seem to characterize so much of "civil rights" advocacy today (as in the case of minority business set-asides and much of affirmative action). Active involvement of our "best and brightest" in the lives of their fellows, and critical appraisal of our community's strengths and weaknesses, will also be necessary. Yet these things will not be forthcoming, so long as politically conscious, articulate, well-educated, and well-positioned Blacks believe that they adequately discharge their community obligations by voting Democratic and regularly denouncing racism. Changing these circumstances will require the empathy, courage, and wisdom of which genuine intellectual leadership is made.

NOTES

1. *Profiles, College Bound Seniors,* 1981, College Entrance Examination Board, New York (1982).
2. See *The Reagan Experiment,* John L. Palmer and Isabelle V. Sawhill, eds., Urban Institute Press, Washington, D.C. (1983).
3. Lester C. Thurow, *The Zero-Sum Society,* Penguin Books (1980).
4. Finish Welch, *"Affirmative Action and Its Enforcement,"* American Economic Review Proceedings (May 1981), tables 1 & 2, p. 129.
5. U.S. Department of Commerce, *Current Population Reports,* Series P-23, no. 107 (1981), table 21.
6. William J. Wilson, *The Declining Significance of Race,* University of Chicago Press, Chicago (1978).
7. Kenneth Clark, "Contemporary Sophisticated Racism," in J. R. Washington, ed., *The Declining Significance of Race: Myth or Reality,* University of Pennsylvania (1980), pp. 99-105.
8. M. L. King, Jr., *Where Do We Go From Here?* Beacon Press, Boston (1968), p. 132.
9. See, for example, Joyce Ladner, *Tomorrow's Tomorrow: The Black Woman,* Doubleday & Company (1970), for such a treatment of the issues of single parenthood.
10. Data cited in this paragraph are from *Statistical Abstract of the United States* (1981), tables 300-312.
11. Op. cit., note 8, p. 125.

PERSPECTIVES ON UNEMPLOYMENT AND POLICY

Nancy S. Barrett

Unemployment rose three percentage points in one year, from 7.4% in the third quarter of 1981 to 10.4% in October 1982. This was the largest yearly increase in unemployment in postwar history. It is inconceivable that any sensible person could attribute this unprecedented increase in our most widely agreed upon measure of economic welfare and performance to anything other than an aggregate demand recession.

In order to prevent unemployment from rising, real gross national product (GNP) must grow by about 2%. Instead, real GNP declined by 3% between October 1981 and October 1982. Industrial production — output in manufacturing and other goods-producing sectors — dropped by 11%. In the second quarter of 1982, the so-called GNP gap — the difference between what the economy was producing in the way of goods and services and what it could have potentially produced at a high-employment level — was 9.6% of GNP, or $320 billion per year. Capacity utilization in manufacturing, according to the Federal Reserve Board, dropped 11 percentage points, from 79.3% to 68.4%, during the same period. In October 1982, capacity utilization in manufacturing stood at its lowest level since the Federal Reserve Board began collecting these data in 1948.

Okun's Law, a relationship developed by the late Arthur Okun of the prestigious Brookings Institution, predicts a rise in unemployment of about 2.25% when real GNP falls by 3%.[1] This alone explains three-quarters of that year's 3% rise in unemployment. Unemployment rose somewhat more than Okun's Law had predicted, primarily because fewer discouraged workers gave up looking for work and dropped out of the labor force than had been typical in postwar recessions. Although there remained some two million such workers who were jobless and who would have taken available work — they were "unemployed" from a conceptual point of view, but were not included in the official statistics — the fact that a high proportion of experienced workers lost their jobs in this recession made the ranks of discouraged workers somewhat smaller than usual. Experienced workers, being eligible for unemployment benefits that require the recipient actively to seek work, were less likely to drop out of the labor force even when discouraged than were inexperienced workers who were not eligible for such benefits.

Of course, stronger-than-expected labor force participation was not a reason for unemployment; rather, it only meant that unemployment was distributed somewhat differently between active job seekers and those who had become discouraged and stopped looking for work. It is important to recognize that higher labor force participation rates in recent years — both as a cyclical and as a trend phenomenon — have been due to a higher propensity for previously employed workers to remain in the labor force after they lose or leave a job, not to a higher rate of new entry. This latter phenomenon, a strengthening of the labor force attachment of workers, is evidence on the positive side of the debate over trends in the work ethic of the U.S. labor force, a debate to which we shall return shortly.

WHAT IS "FULL EMPLOYMENT"?

While most people would concede that increases in unemployment during 1981-82 were due to the recession in aggregate demand, there is less agreement among economists regarding the appropriate long-run target for unemployment. That is, how low can expansionary economic policies bring unemployment before the labor market becomes "tight?"[2] In popular terminology, this unemployment target is called "full employment"; some economists, perhaps hestitant to be judgmental, refer to the NAIRU, that is, the non-accelerating-inflation rate of unemployment.[3]

Most economists used to believe the NAIRU was around 3.5 to 4.0%. They believed this because during the 1950s and 1960s we experienced unemployment rates in this range without inflation accelerating. Ever since the so-called oil shock of 1973, when the price of imported oil quadrupled, unemployment has not fallen below 5%, and has averaged around 7%. Unemployment in 1979, however, fell to 5.8%, but inflation picked up too, leading some economists to the conclusion that the NAIRU was in excess of 6%.[4]

Subscribers to the view that the NAIRU has risen substantially attribute the increase to various structural and institutional factors. Leading explanations are so-called demographic shifts that have increased the representation of youths, women, and generally less-skilled and inexperienced workers who are relatively more prone to unemployment, even in tight labor markets than are adult males.[5] Institutional factors are cited, particularly the growth of unemployment insurance and other transfer payments that require the recipient to seek work while providing a potential financial incentive for him not to take a job. Other adherents to the higher NAIRU view argue that whatever the cause, inflation accelerated in 1973 and again in 1978, when unemployment fell below 5% and 6%, respectively, in those years.

There are excellent arguments against the position that the NAIRU has risen substantially since the late 1960s. On the strictly empirical side, inflation picked up in 1973 and 1978 primarily because of huge oil price increases by the Organization of Petroleum Exporting Countries in those years and, in addition, because of cost-of-living escalators in wage agreements that translated this energy inflation into wage inflation. Wages rose in response to energy shocks, not because labor markets were tight, but because the escalators raised them automatically.

On the theoretical side, it has been said that economies are like bicycles. They operate efficiently only when they go fast — and they operate differently at different speeds.[6] The fact that individuals willingly take up unemployment insurance, disability payments, and other transfers when they cannot find a job does not mean that they would opt for these payments if a good job were available.

Unfortunately, none of our existing transfer programs were in place during periods of labor market tightness, that is, with current payment levels and eligibility criteria. Hence, we do not have the experience necessary to assess their impact on the NAIRU based on actual empirical evidence. Instead, all we are able to do is to simulate how the economy might behave if the unemployment rate were lower than it actually is. However, these simulations must be based on hypothetical conditions, that is, a high demand for labor coupled with the availability of today's income transfer options. Built into such simulations must be some assumptions about the extent to which people would opt for income transfers over a job in tight labor markets. Since we cannot judge this on the basis of experience, the question boils down to whether human motivation to work has changed in any fundamental way in recent years.

Of course, having experienced a decade of extraordinarily high unemployment due to restrictive economic policies, the social stigma attached to receiving unemployment benefits and welfare has gradually lessened.

Last year, over 20 million persons experienced some unemployment, and over 12 million persons received an unemployment benefit payment or a welfare check. With such a large proportion of the population participating in these programs, they would naturally lose some of their stigma. Among the low-income population, participation at some time over a two- or three-year period is practically universal. But it is questionable whether this change in attitudes regarding income transfers reflects a growing aversion to work among Americans, or rather a realistic response to an economic climate in which no jobs are available. In a society where practically all channels for achievement and status are through paid employment, it is unlikely that work incentives have changed in any fundamental way. Rather, ''attitudes'' have adjusted to alleviate the individual guilt and social alienation experienced by the jobless. High levels of anxiety, alcoholism, suicide, child and wife abuse, and other forms of aberrant behavior continue to be associated with unemployment, and there is no evidence from psychological studies that the psychological ''tolerance'' to unemployment has increased in recent years.[7] College students in the 1980s seem to be far more concerned about their future careers than were their counterparts in the 1960s, suggesting at least that the work ethic is still alive and well among the nation's youth — at least among those not forced to rationalize away their total alienation from the social and economic system.

STRUCTURAL EXPLANATIONS OF UNEMPLOYMENT

Finally, a great deal has been said about the effect of so-called relative price changes on unemployment. These include the structural changes resulting from higher energy prices, environmental regulation, foreign competition, and the like that have particularly affected some of our traditional manufacturing industries, like automobiles and steel. To attribute the current high level of unemployment to these changes is again to take the cart before the horse. Economies operate efficiently only at full employment. The economic slack that has been so unwisely allowed to persist during the past decade has greatly reduced the economy's capacity to adjust to the intersectoral shifts in demand that occur when relative prices change. The problem is not the intersectoral shifts, but rather the slack economy that does not provide jobs for laid-off workers in declining sectors. This leads in turn to a mentality that seeks to forestall these changes, resulting in faulty government interventions, like the imposition of trade barriers and inefficient allocative decisions by companies and labor unions. The outcome is a lower rate of growth in real GNP, lower wages, and reduced real income and living standards, added to the loss of potential output occasioned by the recession-induced unemployment.

POLICY IMPLICATIONS

Once it is recognized that unemployment is the outcome of inadequate aggregate demand, and that the NAIRU need not be appreciably higher than in the high-employment decades of the 1950s and 1960s, the policy implications are straightforward. Expansionary aggregate demand measures must be taken. We must return to the posture of the Humphrey-Hawkins Act and the Employment Act of 1946, which mandate policy-makers to be guided first and foremost by the goal of full employment. The red herring of the budget deficit must be exposed as an irrelevant, artificial concept. Inflation is, potentially, a more serious problem, but inflation must be addressed as a separate issue from that of reducing unemployment. The notion that there is necessarily an inverse relationship between inflation and unemployment has been discredited both theoretically and by the facts.[8]

Most wage increases in the past decade have arisen from cost-of-living adjustments; real wages have not risen significantly since 1973. Moreover, cost-of-living escalation is quite unevenly and inequitably distributed across income recipients in our society, so that inflation is having serious, and generally unrecognized, redistributive consequences that work largely to the disadvantage of the working poor.

Government itself has been responsible for many of the inflationary influences that are transmitted by these escalators, through such self-inflicted wounds as farm price supports, trade protection, payroll tax increases, and the like. Addressing the inflation question in the context of a national incomes policy that makes explicit the distributional issues that these inflationary actions are designed to cover up, would be a much more fruitful approach to reducing inflation than is a policy designed to reduce inflation by keeping the economy in a permanent recession.

This is not to say that direct employment programs like public service employment, training, and safety-net welfare measures should be eliminated. These programs have two important functions. First, they can be designed to provide special assistance to workers and potential workers who — because of their age, sex, race, geographic location, or other factors — need help in making the transition from joblessness to regular employment. Second, these programs provide assurance to the unemployed that government is ready, as a last resort, to provide jobs and income support when the system fails. Unless it is willing to serve that role, a growing number of Americans will lose faith in our government and in the economic system it serves.

NOTES

This paper was originally presented at a symposium, "Four Alternative Perspectives on Unemployment and Policy," Vivian Wilson Henderson Lectures in Labor Economics, Clark College, November 18, 1982.

1. Arthur M. Okun, "Potential GNP: Its Measurement and Significance," in Arthur M. Okun, *The Political Economy of Prosperity* (Washington: The Brookings Institution, 1970), pp. 132-145. The original Okun article estimated the responsiveness of unemployment to changes in real output at .33, but this estimate is outdated. A more recent estimate of .45 is found in John A. Tatom, "Economic Growth and Unemployment: A Reappraisal of the Conventional View," *Federal Reserve Bank of St. Louis Review* (October 1978), pp. 16-22.

2. There is no consensus among economists over an exact definition of labor market tightness. A recent collection of papers on the topic is Martin Neil Baily (ed.), *Workers, Jobs, and Inflation* (Washington: Brookings Institution, 1982).

3. Baily, op. cit. Also see, U.S. Department of Labor, *Employment and Training Report of the President, 1979* (Washington: Government Printing Office, 1980), pp. xviii-xx.

4. See, for instance, Michael L. Wachter, "The Changing Cyclical Responsiveness of Wage Inflation," *Brookings Papers on Economic Activity* (1976:1), pp. 115-168.

5. See George L. Perry, "Changing Labor Markets and Inflation," *Brookings Papers on Economic Activity* (1970), pp. 411-441; Martin Neil Baily, "Labor Market Performance, Competition, and Inflation," in *Workers, Jobs, and Inflation,* op. cit., pp. 15-48; and Robert H. Havemann, "Unemployment in Western Europe and the United States: A Problem of Demand, Structure, or Measurement?" *American Economic Review,* LXVIII (May 1978), pp. 44-50.

6. Robert B. Reich, "Making Industrial Policy," *Foreign Affairs,* LX (Spring 1982), pp. 853-881.

7. M. Harvey Brenner, "Assessing the Social Costs of National Unemployment Rates," testimony before the Subcommittee on Domestic Monetary Policy of the Committee on Banking, Finance and Urban Affairs, U.S. House of Representatives, Washington, D.C., August 12, 1982.

8. Arnold Packer and Nancy S. Barrett, "Inflation is New Math," *Washington Post,* March 24, 1980. Comparing the increase in the Consumer Price Index of 13.3% in 1979 with 4.8% in 1976, 6.2 percentage points of the difference was accounted for by energy, interest rates, and food. These were direct effects only. None of these factors were in any way related to unemployment.

REFERENCES

Baily, Martin Neil (ed.). *Workers, Jobs, and Inflation.* Washington: Brookings Institution, 1982.
Barrett, Nancy S. and Morgenstern, Richard D. "Why Do Blacks and Women Have High Unemployment Rates? *Journal of Human Resources,* IX (Fall 1974), 452-464.

Brenner, M. Harvey, "Assessing the Social Costs of National Unemployment Rates." Testimony before the Subcommittee on Domestic Monetary Policy of the Committee on Banking, Finance and Urban Affairs, U.S. House of Representatives, Washington, D.C., August 12, 1982

Havemann, Robert H. "Unemployment in Western Europe and the United States: A Problem of Demand, Structure, or Measurement?" *American Economic Review,* LX-VIII (May 1978), pp. 44-50.

Holt, Charles C. *et al. The Unemployment-Inflation Dilemma: A Manpower Solution.* Washington: Urban Institute, 1970.

Okun, Arthur M. *The Political Economy of Prosperity.* Washington: Brookings Institution, 1970.

Perry, George L. "Changing Labor Markets and Inflation," *Brookings Papers on Economic Activity* (1970), pp. 411-441.

Reich, Robert B. "Making Industrial Policy," *Foreign Affairs,* LX (Spring 1982), pp. 853-881.

Tatom, John A. "Economic Growth and Unemployment: A Reappraisal of the Conventional View," *Federal Reserve Bank of St. Louis Review* (October 1978), pp. 16-22.

Wachter, Michael L. "The Changing Cyclical Responsiveness of Wage Inflation," *Brookings Papers on Economic Activity* (1976:1), pp. 115-168.

MONEY GROWTH AND THE EMPLOYMENT ASPIRATIONS OF BLACK AMERICANS

Everson Hull

Over the past 20 years, considerable attention has been focused on the worsening problem of unemployment among non-white Americans, particularly that of youth. Among congressional actions to address this difficulty were the Economic Opportunity Act of 1964 that established the residential and training program known as Job Corps *and* the Comprehensive Employment and Training Act (CETA-1973) that was aimed at combating long-term, structural unemployment as well as unemployment caused by economic downturns.

Since its inception in 1974, growth in CETA expenditures skyrocketed at a compound annual rate of 44.7% from $1.5 billion in fiscal year 1974 to a peak of $9.5 billion in fiscal year 1978. During 1978 alone, expenditures surged by almost 70%. Since 1978, a number of changes in the eligibility criteria allowed a modest reduction in expenditures and by 1980, the last year of the Carter administration, CETA expenditures showed a slight decline to $8.9 billion.

The accelerated rate of spending for training and related services under CETA did not produce the expected reversal in unemployment patterns that many anticipated. Unemployment for non-whites was 13.2% in 1980, about the same rate that occurred in 1976, and the non-white-white unemployment rate differential widened to 6.8% compared to 6.1% during 1976.[1] Further erosion in non-white employment gains in recent years placed that differential at a record high 9.7% during the first half of 1983.

Attempts to explain these high rates of unemployment among non-white Americans have given very little attention to the effects of (1) cyclic changes in aggregate demand and (2) their key determinants. Recently, a large number of alternative hypotheses have been advanced and empirically tested. Most of the studies have focused on the micro aspects of youth unemployment where the largest share of non-white unemployment is concentrated. These studies do reasonably well in explaining trends in non-white employment during the 1960s, but are less reliable in explaining these trends for subsequent periods.

This study seeks to examine the interrelationship between significant changes in money supply growth and the divergence between non-white and white rates of unemployment. Particular attention is given to episodes of dramatic deceleration in money supply growth during the 1970s and early 1980s and the widening divergence in non-white–white unemployment rates.

We begin below with a review of alternative hypotheses that have been advanced for explaining the determinants of the rise in non-white–white unemployment rate differentials. Next is an examination of recent developments in monetary policy and the effects of these changes on economic activity in general, and employment of non-white Americans in particular. Following that is an examination of the statistical significance of the interrelationships between the "roller-coaster" monetary policy of the Federal Reserve and changes in non-white–white unemployment rate differentials. Finally, a few summary observations are presented.

REVIEW OF ALTERNATIVE THEORIES

Because the problem of non-white unemployment is so largely concentrated on non-white youth, a proliferation of studies appearing in the literature have focused on identifying the main factors precipitating the widening gap between non-white and white unemployment rates among youth. These studies concentrate on the black cohort group aged 16 to 19 whose unemployment rate in August 1983 was 53% compared to 17.4% for Blacks over 20 years of age. Very little attention is given to the separate and tragic problem of black male youth (aged 16 to 19) whose unemployment rate in August 1983 soared to 56.8% and whose employment-to-population ratio declined from 52% in 1954 to 29% in 1980. The data reveal that Blacks over 20 years of age suffer unemployment experiences that are *more closely* in line with similar cohort groups than do blacks under 20 years of age.

Before reviewing a number of competing theories that seek to explain changes in unemployment among non-white American youth and, ipso facto, changes in employment among non-whites, it is important to understand the meaning of these extraordinarily high rates. An attempt is made here to place these high rates in proper perspective.

Traditional statistics on unemployment are not a reliable guide to understanding the special problems of youth. A forthcoming Department of Labor study of trends in youth joblessness during the 1970s highlights a number of obvious though, nonetheless, important differences. Among its key findings are:

- Standard measures of unemployment do not fully characterize the labor market experiences of youth. A close evaluation of the problem indicates that youth joblessness may have less of a social and economic impact than is commonly argued.
- The primary activity of most teenagers is not work but school. In October 1982, more than two-thirds of both black and white teens were enrolled in school. For the year 1982, as a whole, almost half of all unemployed teens were enrolled in school (and more than 90% of these individuals desired only part-time work).
- Only 9% of black teens and 6% of white teens were both out of school and looking for work in 1982, in the midst of a severe recession.
- Over 90% of all black and white teenagers who wanted work (even those in school) gained work experience during 1981.
- Living with parents or relatives provides a built-in safety net for the vast majority of unemployed teens. During 1982, 89% of all white teenagers and 94% of all black teenagers lived with parents or relatives. Very few teens are heads of households with the accompanying financial obligations.

The above discussion is not in any way intended to reduce the significance of the non-white employment problem among youth but rather to place, in proper perspective, the various theories that have been offered for explaining the tragic situation faced by this group. These studies of the youth unemployment problem have typically employed a micro approach for addressing the issue.

Cogan (1982), focusing on the period 1950 to 1970, argues that the underlying forces reducing black teenage employment are (1) the substantial decline in the demand for low-skilled agricultural labor, particularly in the South, and (2) the rise in the real minimum wage.[2] The latter factor, whose coverage expanded to the teenage intensive retail trade and service sectors, prevented the displaced southern Black from being reemployed in the North. The Cogan analysis offers an important contribution to our understanding of the determinants of changes in employment among black Americans for the period 1950 to 1970. However, his results should not be applied to the seventies since there was little migration from the agricultural sector after 1970. Also, his results leave unexplained the relative stability in employment-to-population ratios for other youth cohort groups while comparable ratios for black male youth declined sharply.

The effects of the minimum wage have received considerable attention in the economic literature. These studies have typically produced mixed results. Betsey and Dunson, for example, find that minimum wage legislation has decreased the share of normal employment and increased the vulnerability to cyclical changes in employment for the group most "marginal" to the workforce—teenagers.[3] They also find that minimum-wage legislation resulted in higher wages for the few low-productivity workers who gained employment. By contrast, their findings also suggest that adult whites have been the larger beneficiaries of shifts in the pattern of employment shares resulting from the minimum wage.

Other theories that have sought to address the worsening problem of non-white employment during the 1970s have examined the effects of changes in the military, school enrollment, family structure, the baby boom, welfare expenditures, and the effects of discrimination. These determinants typically explain only a small proportion of the changes in non-white unemployment and are not sufficient for explaining the widening gap between non-white and white unemployment rates that has emerged during the 1970s.

In contradistinction to the above studies that employ a micro approach, there are few studies that adopt a macro approach to the study of trends in non-white unemployment. These studies have sought to examine the employment effects of cyclical changes in economic activity on various cohort groups. However, most of this work takes cyclical changes as given, and does not examine the underlying impulses that produce these changes. The nature of these impulses has important implications for the severity of unemployment that Blacks experience and is especially relevant for the period of the 1970s.

Earlier analysis of the effects of cyclic changes have not sought to relate the underlying impulses behind changes in economic activity to the non-white unemployment problem. Kosters and Welch (1972), using data for the period 1954 to 1968, find that employment for non-whites is more sensitive to changes in economic activity than is employment for whites; and teenagers are found to be more sensitive to changes in economic activity than adults.[4] In a similar vein, Betsey and Dunson (1981) find that for the period 1970 to 1979, teen employment was not significantly affected by cyclical movements in the economy.[5] Their findings suggest that the disemployment effects of the minimum wage increased sharply during the period 1970 to 1979.

Missing from the work of Kosters & Welch and Betsey & Dunson is any attempt to examine the separate effects of specific policy actions on economic activity and the subsequent effects on the employment aspirations of black Americans. The severity of the employment effects may be quite different depending on the form of the impulse. The next section explores the effect of one very important macroeconomic policy impulse on non-white unemployment rates that has been absent from the debate and that has gone largely unexplored in the economic literature.

THE MONEY-EMPLOYMENT NEXUS:
RECENT DEVELOPMENTS

The transmission mechanism for the money-employment causal connection as it relates to black Americans is no different than for any other group. The magnitude of the effects, however, are so profound that this nexus should be an important part of any theory that seeks to explain the employment difficulties of non-whites.

Consider two major instruments of economic policy that may be used in the fight against an *endemic* inflation (1) a contractionary monetary policy and (2) an increase in federal taxes or a reduction in government purchases. Either of these policies would likely produce a reduction in the rate of inflation if pursued over a protracted period and with sufficient vigor, albeit at the expense of some unemployment. (The rise in unemployment may be avoided *if and only if* there is a concomitant rise in productivity.)

As the U.S. government fought a losing battle over a virulent inflation, it became clear to many observers that our disputatious Congress lacked the will to restrain aggregate demand in the face of sluggish growth in output and productivity. The major burden of the fight against inflation, thus, fell on the Federal Reserve.

Throughout most of the 1970s and continuing today, members of the Federal Reserve publicly acknowledged the overriding importance of controlling inflation. Arthur F. Burns and those who succeeded him at the chairmanship have increasingly emphasized that a *gradual* and *persistent* deceleration in the rate of growth of the money supply is a necessary condition for reversing ongoing acceleration in the rate of inflation.

This view, typically embraced by the monetary school of economic thought, holds that restrictive policies pursued by the monetary authorities, particularly during the recent period (1979 to mid-1982), forces a number of involuntary choices on key economic participants, resulting in some moderation in the demand for labor, capital, energy, and other factors of production, causing a deceleration in the prices of these inputs.

The tough, antiinflationary policies of the Federal Reserve enacted in October 1979 raised the price of credit (interest rates), causing a reduction in aggregate demand for goods and services. Interest-rate effects are clearly evident in the case of housing for which high mortgage rates reduce demand restoring some stability to housing prices. Less obvious are the indirect effects of the Fed's actions on energy and other commodity prices. The dramatic decline in the sales of automobiles as well as the demand for gasoline and oil is, at least in part, a result of the recent high automobile finance rates associated with a reduction in the availability of money. The effects of rising interest rates hit hard on interest-sensitive industries (housing, autos and steel) and to a lesser degree the service-related industries where large numbers of Blacks are employed producing a concomitant rise in their unemployment rates.

Of the broad array of government policies directed at influencing the course of economic activity during the 1970s, perhaps none has had a greater adverse effect on the aspirations of black Americans than has the Federal Reserve's conduct of monetary policy. In particular, the "stop-go" pattern of discretionary attempts by the Central Bank to regulate the price and, more recently (beginning in October of 1979), the quantity of money in circulation, in attempting to halt an endemic inflation, have severely frustrated the aspirations of black Americans.

The decline in the rate of inflation has been impressive. The drop has been dramatic, occurring over a relatively short time span. Over a three-year interval, the inflation rate measured by the consumer price index for urban consumers fell from a cyclical peak of 17.2% in the first quarter of 1980 to an average rate of 2.5% for the fiscal year ending July of 1983.

But this improvement has been accomplished at considerable expense. As President Reagan warned in his State of the Union address in January 1981, "progress would be measured in inches, not in feet." Two periods of severe recession have resulted in the highest rates of unemployment for black Americans since 1941, with rates reaching 20.8% of the labor force in December 1982.

The costs in terms of employment are high. Nonetheless, in the absence of a reversal in downward productivity trends, they were inevitable in order to reverse a 15-year pattern of accelerating inflation. The effects of a recession are devastating. It causes tremendous suffering. Unlike sustained and accelerating inflation, however, recession is a cyclical phenomenon that may not seriously weaken the potential growth of the economy over the *long run*. The costs of postpoining a cure for inflation are closely related to the duration of the postponement of that cure. It could be argued that these costs would be lower if disinflation were accomplished in a more orderly fashion and over a somewhat more protracted interval. But such a policy may bring with it additional concerns about a willingness to "stay the course."

The next section examines the statistical interrelationships between the "roller-coaster" monetary policy of the Federal Reserve *and* the dramatic halt to inflation, albeit at the expense of a reduction in aggregate demand and a concomitant rise in non-white–white unemployment rate differentials.

THE MONEY-EMPLOYMENT NEXUS: THE EMPIRICAL EVIDENCE

A perfect one-to-one correspondence between significant monetary decelerations and recessions does not exist. Notwithstanding, there is a very significant and close relationship that suggests that the probability of recession increases significantly with the degree of sharpness of monetary deceleration.

Higgins (1979), for example, using data since 1952, finds that there is a one-to-one relationship between "significant" monetary decelerations and recessions.[6] In establishing the statistical significance of these decelerations in money growth, Hull (1982) incorporates the effects of both the duration and the sharpness of decline in growth rates for five alternative forms of money (M1-B, M1-A, M2, M3, and the monetary base).[7] His statistical comparisons of standardized "Z" statistics (Table 1) show that on a year-over-year basis the 1979 to 1981 deceleration in growth rates for the monetary aggregates has been more protracted than that of any other continuous period of the previous 20 years.

With the exception of growth in M3, which accelerated moderately during 1981, each of the other key monetary aggregates (M1-B, M1-A, M2, and the monetary base) has, since the federal policy change, shown *sustained* deceleration on a year-over-year basis from their long-run paths.

TABLE 1
"Z" Values for Changes in Growth Rates
of the Money Supply[a]

	M1–B	M1–A	Monetary Base	M2	M3
1961	1.223	0.939	0.880	1.018	1.098
1962	0.123	0.299	1.087	0.335	0.320
1963	0.179	0.301	0.456	0.148	0.157
1964	0.398	0.459	0.653	-0.282	-0.252
1965	0.029	0.240	-0.207	0.021	0.012
1966	0.014	0.210	-0.161	-0.636	-0.682
1967	-0.658	-0.172	-0.675	0.076	0.053
1968	1.955	1.381	1.244	0.449	0.193
1969	-0.959	-0.372	-1.272	-0.882	-1.326
1970	-1.766	-0.831	-0.866	-0.928	-0.506
1971	1.929	1.357	2.364	2.965	3.653
1972	0.068	0.250	-0.771	0.064	-0.577
1973	-0.120	0.128	0.514	-1.006	-0.195
1974	-1.866	-0.892	-0.180	-1.459	-1.313
1975	-0.421	-0.093	-0.901	1.141	-0.585
1976	0.502	0.406	-0.291	1.285	0.703
1977	1.176	0.877	0.222	-0.155	0.454
1978	0.160	0.308	0.774	-1.588	-0.330
1979	-0.483	-0.966	-1.156	-0.058	-0.558
1980	-1.291	-0.210	-0.456	-0.083	-0.404
1981[b]	-0.162	-3.483	-2.014	-0.249	0.140

[a]Changes are computed on the basis of first differences in growth rates.

[b]1981 data based on the first 3 quarters only.

SOURCE: Hull, Everson, "Examining the Monetary Causes of the Economic Slowdown," CRS Report #HG 546 U.S., March 1982, p. 12.

Table 2 presents a comparison of the effects of decelerating growth in the monetary indicators on the gross national product gap one year later. The periods identified are selected because of the sharp deceleration in money supply growth that occurred. There is a striking degree of uniformity in these relationships. Sustained periods of declining or slack economic activity are characterized by large increases in the GNP gap

TABLE 2
"Z" Values for Decelerating Money Supply Growth and GNP Gap One Year Later[a]

Period	Ml-B	Ml-A	M2	M3	Monetary Base	Period	GNP[b] GAP
68:IVQ to 69:IVQ	-.303	-.203	-.348	-.758	-.371	69:IVQ to 70:IVQ	2.9
72:IVQ to 74:IQ	-.068	-.028	-.332	-.340	-.212	73:IVQ to 75:1Q	1.3
78:IIIQ to 79:IVQ	-.239	-.159	-.099	-.290	-.119	79:IIIQ to 80:IVQ	4.6
79:IVQ to 81:IIIQ	-.337	-.292	-.149	-.061	-.306	80:IVQ to 82:IIIQ	3.9

[a]"Z" values are computed on the basis of first differences in money supply growth rates.

[b]Represents the percentage point increase in the GNP gap (i.e., ((Potential real GNP - Actual real GNP)/Potential real GNP)*100).

(i.e., actual GNP falls far short of the economy's potential).

Four of these episodes are presented in Table 2: 1969:IVQ to 1970:IVQ; 1973:IVQ to 1975:IQ; 1979:IIIQ to 1980:IVQ; and 1980:IVQ to 1982:IIIQ. Each period of sharp deceleration in economic activity tends to be preceded one year earlier by a sharp deceleration in the rate of money supply growth. Moreover, periods of *sharpest* deceleration in money supply growth tend, on balance, to be followed one year later by a sharp deceleration or stagnation in economic activity causing the economy to operate far short of its potential. This pattern appears to be the case during much of the 1970s and is especially true for the period 1979:IVQ to 81:IIIQ when the Federal Reserve's restrictive policies were pursued most intensely.

The Federal Reserve's sharp deceleration in money supply growth during this period helped produce a reduction in real final demands that held actual GNP well below the productive potential of the economy. During the 1981-82 recession, real GNP remained in the neighborhood of $1.50 trillion with very weak recoveries and very mild contractions from that level. By contrast the Council of Economic Advisers estimated an average potential real GNP during 1981 and 1982 of $1.65 trillion. Thus, the economy experienced a loss in productive potential that averaged $150 billion during 1981 and 1982.

This results in lost job opportunities for all Americans and especially Blacks. The lost output opportunities prevent the economy from generating enough jobs to meet the needs of new entrants into the labor force. Table 3 shows the effect of sharp decelerations in money supply growth

TABLE 3
"Z" Values for Decelerating Money Supply Growth and the
Non-White–White Unemployment Rate Differential Two Years Later[a]

Period	M1–B	M1–A	M2	M3	Monetary Base	Period	Unempl.[b] GAP
68:IVQ to 69:IVQ	-.303	-.203	-.348	-.758	-.371	70:IVQ to 71:IVQ	30.5
72:IVQ to 74:1Q	-.068	-.028	-.332	-.340	-.212	74:IVQ to 76.1Q	27.3
78:IIIQ to 79:IVQ	-.239	-.159	-.099	-.290	-.119	80:IIIQ to 81:IVQ	16.5
79:IVQ to 81:IIIQ	-.337	-.292	-.149	-.061	-.306	81:IVQ to 83:IIQ	29.0

[a]"Z" values are computed on the basis of first differences in money supply growth rates.

[b]Represents the percentage point increase in the nonwhite–white unemployment rate differential.

on the degree of inequality in the distribution of employment opportunities between non-white and white Americans.

A two-year lag is considered here as a reasonable period of time for the full effects of a deceleration in money supply growth to be translated into an increase in unemployment. Our results indicate a strong degree of association between sharp decelerations in money supply growth and a widening of the gap between non-white and white unemployment rates. The two-year acceleration in money supply growth that occurred following the Federal Reserve's change in operating procedures of October 1979 produced a widening of the gap between non-white and white unemployment rates of 29% for the two-year period ending in June 1983. Similar periods of sharp deceleration in money supply growth as occurred during the period 1968:IVQ to 1969:IVQ raised the non-white–white unemployment gap by 30.5%.

The above results may be extended to an examination of the effects of sharp accelerations in money-supply growth. These are shown by Hull (1982) to produce sharp though temporary acceleration in output accompanied by almost certain inflation two years later.[8] A number of disconcerting lags in the hiring process prevent non-whites from being reabsorbed into the mainstream at a sufficiently fast rate to produce a significant narrowing of non-white–white unemployment rate differentials. These findings, which have important implications for government policy, are discussed in the final section.

CONCLUSION

Irrespective of other economic initiatives in the area of fiscal and regulatory policies that may be required, there will not likely be an improvement in the employment situation for black Americans unless policymakers gain a better handle on the conduct of monetary policy. The implication is that the welfare of black Americans tends to improve most when the economy is experiencing high and steady rates of economic growth. The single most important tool for achieving that growth is a highly stable rate of monetary growth that is roughly in line with the long-term growth of the economy.

If we produce too much money for financing projects without raising a commensurate amount of taxes, we will pay the price in terms of higher rates of inflation about two years later. This inflation will tend to be self-perpetuating.

The acceleration in inflation that so develops would eventually produce a public outcry that calls for its reversal. If the Congress fails to exert the will to join in the fight against inflation, the bulk of the burden falls on the Federal Reserve to engineer a painful reduction in the rate of inflation.

Such repetitive patterns produced the ''roller-coaster'' monetary policy of the 1970s. A somewhat more tolerant attitude on the part of the White House towards the Federal Reserve's antiinflation policy allowed a more protracted rate of deceleration in money-supply growth than has been experienced in several years. The rate of deceleration was, however, quite unstable, advancing in fits and spurts. As a consequence, real economic growth was also quite unstable, remaining below the economy's potential and producing a significant displacement of marginal workers—many of whom were non-whites.

While the costs of the Fed's efforts were evidenced by back-to-back recessions in two consecutive years, the benefits are today being reflected in a dramatic reversal of inflationary trends. For the first time in seven postwar recessions, inflation has advanced from a lower base than that associated with the preceding recession. The 15-year trend over which inflation continued to accelerate unabated through economic expansions as well as contractions appears to have been interrupted. Today's broad-based economic recovery shows evidence of advancing without a return to the accelerating trends in inflation of the past 15 years.

To retain these gains, it is important that the Federal Reserve avoid great swings in the monetary aggregates. The Fed should set as its objective a steady and unswerving course. This will have the effect of bringing greater stability to the rate of inflation and would also minimize the severity of recessions. Both of these outcomes are in the best interest of black Americans and serve to narrow the widening gap in unemployment rates among non-whites and whites.

NOTES

1. Unemployment rates for non-white Americans have over the past 30 years remained roughly twice as high as those of white Americans.
2. Cogan, John, "The Decline in Black Teenage Employment: 1950 to 1970," *American Economic Review,* vol. 72, no. 4, September 1982.
3. Betsey, C., and Dunson B., "Federal Minimum Wage Laws and Employment of Minority Youth," *American Economic Review,* vol. 71 (May 1981).
4. Kosters, M., and Welch, Finis, "The Effects of the Minimum Wage on the Distribution of Changes in Aggregate Employment," *American Economic Review,* June 1972.
5. Ibid.
6. Higgins, Bryon, "Monetary Growth and Business Cycles," *Economic Review,* Federal Reserve Bank of Kansas City, April 1979.
7. Hull, Everson, "Examining the Monetary Causes of the Economic Slowdown," CRS Report #HG546, U.S., March 1982. M1-A consists of currency and coin plus commercial bank demand deposits held by the nonbank public including those held by foreign banks and official institutions. M1-B consists of M1-A plus automated transfer service (ATS) and negotiable order withdrawal (NOW) accounts and other checkable deposits at all depository institutions. M2 consists of M1-B plus savings and small time deposits, overnight RPs and money market mutual finds. M3 consists of M2 plus large time deposits and term RPs. The monetary base consists of: (1) member bank reserves at the Federal Reserve Banks, (2) currency in circulation (currency held by the public and in the vaults of commercial banks), and (3) an adjustment for reserve requirement ratio changes. The *major source* of the adjusted monetary base is Federal Reserve credit.
8. Ibid.

ECONOMIC GROWTH, STRUCTURAL CHANGE, AND THE RELATIVE INCOME STATUS OF BLACKS IN THE U.S. ECONOMY, 1947-78

Donald J. Harris

A great deal of attention has been given in recent years to the changing economic status of the black population in the United States. Striking changes have in fact occurred in the position of Blacks relative to whites, as measured, for instance, by the relative income position of the two groups. This position showed a marked increase during the period of the mid 1960s to mid 1970s. Similarly, a significant deterioration has occurred in the past few years. In seeking to provide an explanation of these observed changes, much of the existing analysis has tended to focus on a set of factors related to the technical-productive characteristics of the black population, as represented by a measure of human capital, or on demographic characteristics related to the size, age, and sex composition of the household unit, or on both (see Haworth, et al., 1975; Weiss, 1970; Smith and Welch, 1978).

Whatever may be the actual insights that have been obtained from this particular approach, it is evident that the factors upon which it focuses are essentially of a microeconomic character and partial in their scope of operation. As such, they must be considered to operate within a broader process taking place in the economy as a whole and to derive their significance from the workings of that process. It becomes necessary, therefore, to look to the general features of that larger process and to the specific conditions that are at work within it in order to provide a systematic account of the factors that explain the relative position of blacks.

The research reported here represents a preliminary effort to propose such a wider framework of analysis and to examine its empirical significance in explaining the changing economic position of the black popula-

tion. The focus of analysis is on the post–World War II period of development in the U.S. economy, specifically 1947-1978. This entire period
constitutes a sufficiently long experience of fairly coherent tendencies in
cyclical movements, in overall economic growth, and in structural
change to provide an appropriate empirical context for such an analysis. It
is also a period for which continuous and consistent time series data on
the income and employment status of the black population are available,
making it possible to carry out a long-term analysis. However, the level
of the analysis must still be highly aggregative for reasons of lack of
sufficiently disaggregated data. The econometric analysis used here is
highly simplified and tentative, reflecting the preliminary nature of this
effort. Nevertheless, the results point to some interesting patterns that are
worthy of deeper study with more sophisticated methods and richer data.

ANALYTICAL FRAMEWORK

The essential core of the conception that motivates this study is the idea
that the relative economic position of Blacks is to be understood as the
outcome of a dynamic process taking place in the economy as a whole. In
general terms, it may be referred to as a process of *uneven development.*
This process has a number of specific characteristics that are crucially
relevant for understanding the position of Blacks. First is its cyclical character, which takes the form of a succession of booms and recessions. In
the course of this cyclical movement, sharp fluctuations occur in output,
employment, and income, with different consequences for different economic groups. Second, a characteristic feature of the process is that it is a
process of structural transformation of the economy. This is manifested in
the fact that different sectors, regions, industries, and firms expand at
different rates, in accordance with underlying differences in the rate and
pattern of technical change, in the rate of capital accumulation, and in the
evolution of product demand. Finally, the process also has a political
dimension insofar as the possibilities of collective action within and
among different social groups to seek out and win economic gains
through the political process may improve or worsen from one period to
another.

It is presumed that these features of the process are necessarily inter-
linked. It would be the purpose of a theory to identify these links, to give
a precise analytical specification of the general process, and to derive the
particular ways in which it operates to determine the economic position
of blacks. Such a theory, if it existed, would be extraordinarily complex,

reflecting the complexities of the process itself. Suffice it to say here that a fully developed theory of this nature does not now exist. What we have is a limited understanding of various economic aspects of the process. Least understood of all are the links between the economic and political dimensions of the process. Moreover, very little theoretical work has been done to show exactly how the macrostructural forces impinge on the economic position of Blacks.

 In the absence of such a broadly based theory that would enable the formulation of a completely specified model, it is necessary to proceed in a more limited way. In other related work, I am attempting to construct a theoretical analysis of some aspects of the process. For present purposes, attention is directed here to outlining a set of factors that, in the light of this broader framework of analysis, are hypothesized to be the crucial factors operating in the postwar period to account for changes in the relative economic status of Blacks. An effort is made to assess the empirical significance of these factors through statistical analysis of the available time series data using single-equation least squares regression methods.

HYPOTHESES

The role of cyclical factors in accounting for changes in the economic position of blacks has been widely noted in the literature (see Swinton, 1970; Freeman, 1973, 1981; Thurow, 1969; Rasmussen, 1970; Ashenfelter, 1970; Kniesner, et al. 1978; Reich, 1981). There are important questions that this begs about exactly how these factors are to be represented quantitatively and through what mechanisms they work. In keeping with common practice, it is assumed here that these factors are expressed in two variables: the rate of growth of GNP, and the overall rate of unemployment. The former is presumed to have a positive influence on the relative position of Blacks, the latter a negative influence. Both variables are, in some sense, an index of the state of aggregate demand, but must be supposed to operate in separate and independent ways, one via the product market, the other directly through the labor market.

In particular, it may be argued that, in high-growth periods when aggregate demand is strong, firms are realizing productivity gains both through increased utilization of existing plants and equipment and through investment in more productive methods. At such times, workers as a whole obtain wage and employment increases (the latter depending on the strength of the employment effect generated by the twin forces of output and productivity growth). Correspondingly, Blacks may win relative gains in employment and income, depending on their relative bargaining strength, which may improve as firms face improved product markets. In the downturn, the reverse situation occurs.

This effect may be compounded by certain structural properties of the economy related to differences between what I have characterized elsewhere as the petty-capital sector and the corporate-capital sector (Harris, 1972, 1978). The significant difference between them, for present purposes, is that the petty-capital sector produces product types that have much higher cyclical variability than products of the corporate capital sector. Insofar as employment of Blacks is proportionately greater in the petty capital sector, cyclical movements in output would have correspondingly greater impact on the income position of Blacks.

The unemployment variable expresses the direct role of labor market conditions, or the particular ways in which demand for labor is filtered through the existing employment practices developed by firms and unions. Two such conditions may be considered relevant here. The first is the subordinate status that black labor occupies with the "reserve-army" of unemployed labor insofar as Blacks form a disproportionately large part of the unemployed and are usually the "last hired and first fired." This means that a decline in the rate of unemployment would improve the relative income position of Blacks, and vice versa. The second is what might be called the employment-discrimination effect. In particular, it is probably the case that the degree of discrimination in employment increases as the labor market slackens and, in defensive reaction, organized groups of white workers increasingly resist inroads by Blacks into the shrinking pool of available jobs. It diminishes as the labor market tightens, both because of reduced resistance of white workers and unions to Blacks and because of increased competition among firms for labor. The first of these conditions presumably acts immediately as labor demand changes. The second is likely to operate with a lag.

So far as long-term structural factors are concerned, a significant factor in the postwar experience of the black population, which has also been widely noted, is the large-scale migration of Blacks from the South to the North and West (see Weiss & Williamson, 1972; Gwartney, 1970; Adams & Nestel, 1976; Masters, 1975; Johnson & Campbell, 1981; Reich, 1981). But behind the fact of regional migration itself lies the ongoing process of structural transformation of the economy, which gives rise to sectoral shifts in production and employment as relative contraction occurs in some sectors and expansion in others. It is this complex process of structural change with its associated shifts in employment patterns that is in part expressed in regional migration but has to be considered as a separate and independent factor. Viewed in broad terms, this process reveals a number of distinguishable components. Perhaps the most striking of these is the transformation of agriculture, which releases labor from agricultural production for employment in industry and services. The second is the ongoing transformation within nonagricultural activities as different sectors expand relatively to others. Two significant features of this non-agricultural transformation in the postwar period are the expansion of service-sector employment relative to manufacturing within the private sector and the expansion of public-sector employment relative to private. A third component of structural transformation, accompanying all of these other changes, is the changing occupational and skill composition of the labor force.

It is to be expected that this general process taking place in the economy as a whole would have measurable impact on the relative position of Blacks. In fact, the available data show significant changes in the regional, industrial, and occupational location of Blacks over the entire postwar period. It is appropriate to assume that these changes conform to a pattern of interregional, intersectoral, and interoccupational mobility of black labor that is generated by the underlying tendencies of structural transformation. We may conceive of this as a kind of dynamic *diffusion process* of black labor arising from the absorption/displacement effect of changes taking place in different sectors of the economy. This diffusion process, in turn, may be considered to have two dimensions: (1) *lateral mobility,* consisting of the absorption of more and more Blacks into similar positions in terms of income and occupational status in the same or different industries, and (2) *upward mobility,* consisting of movement across different occupations and industries into higher income positions.

Viewed historically, the diffusion process of Blacks consists of an initial phase of movement out of agricultural activities located predominantly in the South into nonagricultural activities located in urban areas both in the South and in the North. What is significant here is not so much the fact of spatial migration per se, which may be either a matter of rural-urban or South-North migration. Typically, it consists of both of these in different stages of the movement. More significant is the fact that the movement occurs between different sectors of economic activity, with associated differences in income and occupational status. Within nonagricultural activities, there is a complex pattern of movement of Blacks into different sectors and occupations. Starting at particular entry points, this movement takes the form of concentration at initial points of entry as well as movement into new locations.

Mobility between agriculture and industry is in itself a form of upward mobility, hence a factor contributing to improvement in the position of Blacks, insofar as it represents a continuing absorption of new entrants displaced from agricultural activities with lower income and occupational status. Even so, it would by itself represent only a one-time gain for those who make the transition. For Blacks as a group, any improvement arising from this source asymptotically diminishes as the black labor force employed in agriculture declines. Therefore, it is only upward mobility within nonagricultural activities that is capable of sustaining continued improvement for Blacks. Furthermore, such upward mobility must occur at a rate greater than that of whites if it is to result in improvement of the position of Blacks relative to that of whites. Viewed in such relative terms, there may in fact occur downward mobility of Blacks over time despite absolute gains in income and occupational status.

Identification of the particular factors determining lateral and upward mobility of blacks within nonagricultural activities requires close study of the sorting mechanism that allocates labor to different slots in the economy. It is obviously not a random process conforming to the usual conception of a pure competitive labor market. A plausible case can be made on theoretical grounds, and supported in part by some empirical evidence, that it is tied up with such economic factors as industrial market structure, the life cycle of firms and industries, the organizational and technical structure of production activity within firms, the size of firms, the growth rate of firms and industries, and so on. It is associated also with the extent of unionization in different industries and specific practices of different unions. Furthermore, the operation of this mechanism is undoubtedly influenced by government policy and employment practices of the state itself. The neoclassical theory of discrimination is one conception of a type of sorting mechanism based on preferences or tastes of utility maximizing agents, but this has proved to be inadequate. The idea of "labor market segmentation," proposed by some as a characteristic feature of the American economy, also implicitly assumes the existence of a type of sorting mechanism, but this idea has not been well grounded either theoretically or empirically. Elsewhere I have suggested that it may be useful to think of the sorting mechanism in terms of differences in the dynamic behavior of different sectors of capital, broadly identified as the petty-capital sector and the corporate capital sector (Harris, 1972, 1978).

Deeper study of this mechanism is evidently required. On an empirical level, much can be learned from a disaggregated study of the specific historical pattern of the diffusion process of Blacks throughout the economic system. But, for present purposes, this problem is approached in a more limited way. In particular, it is assumed that the mechanism of allocation of labor to different slots operates to determine the extent and direction of the influence of the process of structural change on the relative position of Blacks. This process is, in turn, represented by movement in the following indices:

1. Regional composition of the total employed labor force, measured by the ratio of employment in the North and West to employment in the South. This variable expresses the influence of purely regional shifts in production and employment.
2. The ratio of private-sector nonagricultural employment to agricultural employment. This expresses the role of sectoral, as distinct from regional, shifts in production and employment, specifically as between the broad categories of agricultural and nonagricultural activities.
3. The ratio of private-sector nonindustrial employment (or "services") to industrial employment. This represents the role of structural shifts within private nonagricultural activities, specifically as between the two broad groups of industrial activities and services.
4. The ratio of government employment to total private-sector nonagricultural employment, which represents the direct influence of employment in the state sector.
5. The ratio of employment in "high-level" occupations to employment in other occupations. This provides a measure of the role of upward mobility across occupations.

It is proposed here to measure the impact of the process of structural change on the relative position of Blacks by introducing these indices as explanatory variables. From these measures, it is possible also to assess the quantitative significance of the sorting mechanism in mediating the process of structural change.

A factor that has been found by other studies to be significant in explaining the changing status of Blacks is the relative growth of human capital invested in the black labor force. These studies have mostly been carried out at a partial-equilibrium microeconomic level. There are complex problems in assessing the exact role of this factor even at that level. These problems are compounded at the aggregative macrolevel of this study. Nevertheless, as a first approximation, explicit consideration is given to this factor through introduction of the ratio of average years of schooling of Blacks and whites as an independent variable. This variable need not be taken to represent a technical-productive relationship as in the usual human-capital interpretation. Instead, it may be taken as a measure of the cost of reproduction of the workers' laboring capacity, a cost that must be met by the wage received insofar as the labor market is reasonably competitive.

It is assumed that, except for this schooling factor, viewed as a cost of reproduction or minimum supply price of labor, other supply considerations have no unambiguous and measurable effect on the relative position of Blacks in the long term. If there is any such effect, it operates through the size of the reserve-army of unemployed. It is therefore captured in the unemployment variable.

Finally, account must be taken of the role of political factors in determining the relative position of Blacks. For a large part of the period under study, there was intense political activity associated with emergence of the Civil Rights movement acting on a national level to effect political, legal, and economic changes in favor of Blacks. Landmark events that give a time profile to this process of political development are the Brown decision of the Supreme Court in 1954 and the Civil Rights Act of 1964. The buildup of political pressures occurring in this earlier phase set the stage for an ensuing phase of opening educational and economic opportunities. This process might be expected to have a measurable impact on the relative position of Blacks (cf. Freeman, 1981; Levin, 1979). This hypothesis is incorporated into the analysis through introduction of a dummy variable that takes the value of 0 for the years 1947-1965 and 1 for 1966-1978, allowance being made for a time lag before the buildup of political pressures begins to take economic effect.

The dependent variable in this analysis is taken to be the relative position of Blacks and whites as measured both by the black-white median income ratio and by the black-white ratio of median earnings (wages and salaries). Within both categories, distinction is made between the relative status of families and that of males and females, respectively. It is presumed that different factors affect families compared with individuals, as also males compared with females. These differences, if significant, should show up in the regression results. It must be presumed also that different factors affect earnings as compared with income. As between these two dependent variables, the major components of the difference are property income and to a lesser extent transfer payments. Systematic treatment of this difference would therefore require explicit consideration of the determinants of income from property and from transfer payments. As a first step, these complications may be ignored. It could be assumed that, at least for Blacks, the factors that affect earnings necessarily affect property income and in the same direction. This is warranted by the fact that most black business enterprises have their base of operation in black communities and correspondingly derive a large part of their incomes from the multiplier effects of expenditure from black earnings.

REGRESSION MODEL

The preceding considerations lead to adoption of a regression model specified in terms of the following equations:

$$y_j = a_j + \sum_{i=1}^{i=9} b_i x_i + e_j \, , j = 1, \ldots , 5$$

where

y_1 = Ratio B/W (Black/White) median income of families.
y_2 = Ratio B/W median income of males.
y_3 = Ratio B/W median income of females.
y_4 = Ratio B/W median earnings of males.
y_5 = Ratio B/W median earnings of females.
x_1 = Overall rate of unemployment, lagged one year.
x_2 = Rate of growth of GNP (deflated).
x_3 = Ratio employment in north and west to employment in south.
x_4 = Ratio nonagricultural to agricultural employment.
x_5 = Ratio nonindustrial to industrial employment (private sector).
x_6 = Ratio government to private nonagricultural employment.
x_7 = Ratio high-level to low-level occupations.
x_8 = Ratio B/W years of schooling.
x_9 = Dummy variable: 1947-65 = 0, 1966-78 = 1.
a_j = Constant.
e_j = Error term.

These equations were estimated using ordinary single-equation least squares methods. The results are reported and discussed in the following sections.

TABLE 1
Regression Results, for Simplified Model, 1948-78
(t-ratios in parentheses)

Independent Variables	Dependent Variables				
	y_1 Family Income	y_2 Male Income	y_3 Female Income	y_4 Male Earnings	y_5 Female Earnings
a	0.5531	0.5165	0.4335	0.5377	0.2621
x_1 (unemployment rate)	-1.5793 (-3.7)	-1.2365 (-2.2)	-1.7634 (-2.3)	-0.4993 (-0.7)	-0.2434 (-0.2)
x_2 (GNP growth rate)	0.2686 (1.4)	0.4256 (1.7)	0.1289 (0.4)	0.2370 (0.8)	-0.1596 (-0.3)
Time	0.0054 (9.8)	0.0053 (7.1)	0.0207 (20.6)	0.0058 (6.4)	0.0234 (13.2)
R^2	0.78	0.65	0.95	0.64	0.90
d	1.12	0.86	1.74	0.87	0.37

THE RESULTS

It is interesting to consider, first of all, a simplified model in which the two cyclical variables, x_1 and x_2, and a time trend are specified as the independent variables, all others being eliminated. This simple specification has been commonly employed in other studies. The regression results for this model are presented in Table 1. The estimated coefficients for the two cyclical variables have the expected sign in all cases, excepting the case of female earnings, where these coefficients are not statistically significant anyway. In general, the cyclical variables are significant in the income equations but not in the earnings equations. As between the two cyclical variables, the unemployment rate, x_1, generally does better than the GNP growth rate, x_2, in explaining variations in income. In all cases, the coefficient of time is positive and highly significant, confirming the general impression that there are significant long-term trend factors at work during the sample period to determine variations in earnings and income.

Consider next the full model. Estimation of the complete equations showed many of the coefficients to be statistically insignificant despite a high value of R^2. This was taken to suggest the presence of a multicollinearity problem. In order to get around this problem, a backward elimination procedure was adopted and supplemented with forward selection

TABLE 2
Regression Results, from Applying Elimination Procedure, 1948-78
(t-ratios in parentheses)

Independent Variables	Dependent Variables				
	y_1 Family Income	y_2 Male Income	y_3 Female Income	y_4 Male Earnings	y_5 Female Earnings
a	0.5365	1.5968	-0.2462	2.0300	1.8526
x_1 (unemployment rate)	-0.6365 (-2.2)	-1.7057 (-4.1)			
x_2 (GNP growth rate)		0.5586 (3.1)			
x_3 (regional employment)					
x_4 (nonagr. employment)	0.0033 (2.4)	0.0100 (9.5)	0.0124 (3.4)	0.0180 (5.8)	0.0354 (28.6)
x_5 (service employment)				-0.5770 (2.9)	
x_6 (govt. employment)			4.7483 (3.8)		
x_7 (occupation mobility)		-1.8743 (-3.3)		-2.1418 (-3.2)	-2.9175 (-3.7)
x_8 (schooling)					
x_9 (dummy variable)	0.0481 (2.8)				
R^2	0.89	0.83	0.95	0.83	0.98
d	1.91	2.04	1.61	2.07	1.74

to check for significance of eliminated variables. In this way it was possible to arrive at an equation with the best overall fit as judged by three tests: the value of R^2 (adjusted for degrees of freedom), t-ratios of the estimated coefficients, and the Durbin-Watson d-statistic. This procedure introduces other problems of its own, such as the possibility of specification error, but this was judged not to be serious. Table 2 gives the regressions resulting from this procedure.

The cyclical variables now drop out of the earnings equations for males and females as well as the female income equation. Their effect shows up most strongly in the equation for male income. In the case of family income, the cyclical effect is confined to the influence of the unemployment variable. From these results and those of the simplified model, it would seem, then, that cyclical factors do have an influence on the relative status of Blacks but their influence is significant only for male income and family income. Their influence on earnings appears to be quite insignificant.

As to the role of long-term-trend factors, one variable turns out to be uniformly insignificant for all dependent variables and is eliminated by the elimination procedure. That variable is x_3, a measure of the regional migration effect. In contrast, x_4, the measure of the shift effect from agriculture into nonagricultural activities, is highly significant and positive in all cases. One may infer from this result that it is the shift from agriculture to nonagricultural activities, rather than spatial or regional migration per se, that has been the significant factor contributing to improvement in the relative status of Blacks. It appears, also, that this agricultural shift effect is the single most important influence operating in the sample period to determine the relative status of Blacks. This is evident from the fact that it is the only independent variable that remains significant across all dependent variables.

As to the influence of factors operating within nonagricultural employment, some of these appear to have a strongly negative effect. In particular, the variable x_7, representing changes in high-level relative to low-level occupations, has a negative sign for all three cases of male income and earnings and female earnings. Similarly, x_5, representing changes in service-sector employment relative to other nonagricultural activities, has a negative sign for male earnings. Thus, it may be inferred that these particular changes are associated with a tendency towards downward mobility for Blacks relative to whites. On the other hand, changes in public-sector employment have a positive effect, but only in the case of female income.

The role of the dummy variable, x_9, turns out to be highly significant and positive in the regression equation for family income, though not so much for individual income and earnings. It is evident that, in the case of family income, data points divide sharply into two distinct clusters, the division occurring between 1965 and 1966. Male income and earnings display a similar though less distinct pattern. For female income and earnings, on the other hand, there is a fairly smooth and continuous rise over the whole period, with a tendency to flattening out (even to decreasing, in the case of female income) in the last few years. At least in the case of family and male income, then, these tests suggest that a significant structural shift occurred round about the middle 1960s causing a significant increase in the relative position of Blacks. A wide range of particular and concrete factors could no doubt be associated with this effect, from equal opportunity programs, to government transfer payments and loans to small business. It is presumed here that they derive in large part from the build-up of political pressures occurring throughout the earlier period and taking full effect as of the mid 60's. These findings may be considered to give some limited support to this view.

SCHOOLING

Special attention was given to the role of schooling, in part because of the importance that has been assigned to this factor in recent discussions. This factor was considered, first, by extending the simplified model with the two cyclical variables and time so as to include both the schooling variable, x_8, and the agricultural shift variable, x_4. The results of estimating this extended model are presented in Table 3. It is evident that, in this model, the agricultural shift effect continues to be highly significant in all cases except male and female income. And only in those two cases does the schooling variable turn out to be significant.

A second approach adopted was to employ the elimination procedure described above to check for significance of the schooling variable. Only in the two cases of male and female income did the schooling variable fail to be eliminated, all other cases yielding the same results as reported in Table 2. The results for these two cases are presented in Table 4. The coefficient of the schooling variable is positive and highly significant in both cases. The agricultural shift effect remains significant for female income, but is displaced by schooling in the case of male income.

These results could be taken to suggest that schooling has a strong influence on income of males and females and may be a strong competitor of the agricultural shift effect, at least in the case of male income. However, this inference would be troublesome and paradoxical if one adopted the human-capital interpretation of the schooling variable. That interpretation predicts a unique and direct role of schooling in determining earnings. But the effect found here for schooling is limited to income, and no significant effect is found in the case of earnings for both males and females. If, on the other hand, one adopts the interpretation of schooling proposed above, as determining a minimum supply-price of labor that need not be binding at all times and in all cases, then this finding is not especially disturbing. Insofar as no significant effect of schooling on earnings appears, it would mean simply that other factors have been sys-

TABLE 3
Regression Results, for Extended Model with Schooling Variable, 1948-78
(t-ratios in parentheses)

Independent Variables	Dependent Variables				
	y_1 Family Income	y_2 Male Income	y_3 Female Income	y_4 Male Earnings	y_5 Female Earnings
a	0.5411	0.1933	−0.0847	0.3975	0.1496
x_1 (unemployment rate)	−1.1379 (−2.8)	−0.4437 (−1.1)	−0.2865 (−0.3)	0.3815 (0.7)	1.7248 (2.2)
x_2 (GNP growth rate)	0.1148 (0.7)	0.1623 (0.9)	−0.3190 (−0.8)	−0.0628 (−0.3)	−0.8428 (−2.8)
x_4 (non-agr. employment)	0.0113 (4.3)	0.0080 (1.6)	0.0084 (1.4)	0.0174 (2.7)	0.0481 (9.7)
x_8 (schooling)	−0.0496 (−0.2)	0.4884 (2.0)	0.7549 (2.2)	0.1236 (0.4)	−0.1091 (−0.4)
Time	−0.0026 (−0.9)	−0.0074 (−3.2)	0.0030 (0.4)	−0.0093 (−3.0)	−0.0122 (−1.8)
R^2	0.86	0.84	0.96	0.81	0.98
d	2.06	2.08	2.03	1.83	1.98

tematically at work in the sample period to determine earnings. Some of these other factors have been identified in this analysis.

As to the significance found for schooling in the income equation for males and females, an intuitive explanation would be that nonwage income of Blacks has grown relatively to that of whites along with observed increases in schooling, because of a corresponding growth of saving and property ownership among the educated higher-income group of the black population. There is independent evidence to suggest increasing quantitative significance of such a group among Blacks. But it would require further empirical investigation to test for the exact role of this factor in explaining the results obtained here.

CONCLUSION

The preceding analysis shows that it is possible to give a consistent and meaningful account of postwar changes in the relative position of Blacks as related to broad macrostructural forces operating in the economy as a whole. Of these, perhaps the most commonly recognized are cyclical

TABLE 4
Regression Results, with Significant Effect of Schooling Variable after
Applying Elimination Procedure
(t-ratios in parentheses)

Independent Variables	Dependent Variables	
	y_2 Male Income	y_3 Female Income
a	0.3672	-0.1814
x_4 (non-agr. employment)		0.0102 (3.1)
x_5 (service employment)	-0.3157 (-2.5)	
x_6 (govt. employment)	-2.2967 (-4.2)	
x_8 (schooling)	0.9814 (8.3)	0.8677 (5.0)
R^2	0.88	0.96

forces associated with fluctuations in aggregate output and employment. Some support is found here for the role of these forces, though the strength of their effect varies as between earnings and income and between individuals and families. But quite apart from such cyclical factors, there are other powerful factors, of an economic as well as political nature, that have operated to influence the position of Blacks. This analysis has succeeded in isolating some of these other factors.

They include a broad set of forces related to the changing structure of employment in the economy as a whole. The most significant of these is the shift of employment from agricultural to nonagricultural activities. This shift, in turn, reflects the operation of push factors associated with long-term transformation of agricultural production and the pull factors of growth in nonagricultural activities. The shift, so long as it has continued, has had a significant positive effect on the relative position of Blacks through the upward mobility that it generates. Of course, being a one-time transition, it cannot be expected to sustain continued improvement for Blacks.

As regards changes taking place within nonagricultural activities, they have had mostly negative effects. In particular, the growth of services relative to traditional industrial activities (manufacturing and transportation) has had a negative influence, noticeably on the relative position of males. Similarly, the growth of high-level occupations has had a negative influence on the position of males, in terms of both income and earnings, and on females in terms of earnings. The only significant positive effect has come from the influence of changes in public sector employment, and this only for female income.

Regional or spatial migration has been commonly regarded as a significant factor influencing the relative position of Blacks. It appears from the analysis presented here that the migration variable has no independent influence of its own. Whatever influence it might have is captured in other variables related to the structural transformation taking place in the economy. It is therefore to be viewed simply as a proxy for these other variables. Insofar as it is only a proxy for these variables, then, what is of interest for analysis is precisely the character of the underlying changes that those variables represent and the direction of their influence on the relative position of Blacks. In this respect, the findings presented here are of special interest. In particular, the wave of migration that occurred in the sample period can be regarded as largely linked to the shift of labor from agriculture into nonagricultural activities. This shift had a positive effect precisely because of the upward mobility associated with it. However, if regional migration were to continue, it would now be associated largely with regional shifts in nonagricultural employment since the shift out of agriculture would have already run its course. But the movement of labor between sectors and occupations within nonagricultural activities does not appear to have a corresponding upward-mobility effect, in terms of the relative position of Blacks, as did the shift out of agriculture. It follows, therefore, that migration by itself cannot be relied upon to continue to bring about improvement in the position of Blacks. This conclusion undercuts the optimism that has been expressed for the potential of the recent trend towards black migration to the South in improving the relative status of Blacks. This recent trend supports the view that black labor does move in response to broad structural changes in the economy (specifically, in response to recent growth of manufacturing and services in the South) but that movement need not be associated with significant *upward* mobility.

These results suggest that there is a sorting process at work here, within the broad grouping of nonagricultural activities, in such a way that, as some sectors and occupations expand relatively to others, Blacks are drawn into locations that are relatively inferior in terms of income and occupational status compared to the positions occupied by whites. The only exception to this general tendency occurs within the sphere of government activity where, as is known also from other evidence, employment practices operate more favorably to Blacks than in the private sector. The specific mechanisms through which this sorting process operates at the microlevel requires deeper investigation.

Finally, this analysis indicates a significant role for the political pressures that emerged in the early part of the period in bringing about the improvements for Blacks that showed up in the later part of the period. These pressures now appear to have weakened considerably in the past few years. One may therefore expect that, coupled with the role of cyclical and long-term structural factors, this is likely to bring about a deterioration in the position of Blacks in the period immediately ahead.

NOTE

This research was supported in part by a grant from the National Institute of Education through the Institute for Research on Educational Finance and Governance at Stanford University. The author is grateful to Henry M. Levin for helpful coordination, to Reginald Nugent for research assistance, and to Penney Jordan for computer programming. My thanks also to Thomas D. Boston and William A. Darity, Jr., for penetrating comments that will improve my subsequent efforts in this area.

DATA SOURCES

1. y_1, y_2, y_3, from U.S. Bureau of the Census, *Current Population Reports,* series P-60, no. 123, tables 11, 65.

2. y_4, y_5, 1947-1949, from U.S. Bureau of the Census, *Current Population Reports,* no. 5, p. 29, no. 6, p. 29, no. 7, p. 36; 1950-1970, from U.S. Bureau of the Census, *Historical Statistics of the U.S. from Colonial Times to 1970,* p. 304; 1971-1978, from U.S. Bureau of the Census, *Current Population Reports,* nos. 85, 90, 97, 101, 105, 114, 118, 123.

3. x_2, from U.S. President's Office, *Economic Report of the President, 1980,* tables B-1 and B-3.

4. x_1, x_3, x_4, x_5, x_6, x_7, from U.S. Department of Labor, *Employment and Training Report of the President,* 1965, tables A-10, D-1; *Employment and Training Report of the President, 1980,* tables A-1, A-16, C-1, D-1. For x_5, the numerator is the sum of Mining, Construction, Manufacturing, Transportation, and Public Utilities; the denominator is the sum of Wholesale and Retail Trade, Finance, Insurance and Real Estate, and Services. For x_7, the numerator is the sum of Professional and Technical, Managers and Administrators, Sales Workers, Craft and Kindred Workers, and Operatives; the denominator is the sum of Clerical Workers and Service Workers.

5. x_8, 1948-1975, from Freeman (1981); 1976-1979, from U.S. Department of Labor, *Handbook of Labor Statistics,* 1980, table 68, pp. 137-38.

REFERENCES

A. Adams and G. Nestel, "Interregional Migration, Education and Poverty in the Urban Ghetto: Another Look at Black-White Earnings Differentials," *Review of Economics and Statistics* 68 (May 1976): 156-66.

O. Ashenfelter, "Changes in Labor Market Discrimination Over Time," *Journal of Human Resources* 5 (fall 1970): 404-30.

R. B. Freeman, "Changes in the Labor Market for Black Americans, 1948-72," *Brookings Papers on Economic Activity* 1 (1973): 67-131.

R. B. Freeman, "Black Economic Progress after 1964: Who Has Gained and Why?," in *Studies in Labor Markets,* ed. S. Rosen (Chicago: University of Chicago Press, 1981), 247-94.

J. Gwartney, "Changes in the Nonwhite/White Income Ratio — 1939-67," *American Economic Review* 60 (December 1970): 872-83.

D. J. Harris, "The Black Ghetto as 'Internal Colony': A Theoretical Critique and Alternative Formulation," *Review of Black Political Economy* 2 (summer 1972): 3-33.

D. J. Harris, "Capitalist Exploitation and Black Labor: Some Conceptual Issues," *Review of Black Political Economy* 8 (winter 1978): 133-51.

J. G. Haworth, J. Gwartney, and C. Haworth, "Earnings, Productivity, and Changes in Employment Discrimination During the 1960's," *American Economic Review* 65 (March 1975): 158-68.

D. Johnson and R. Campbell, *Black Migration in America* (Durham: Duke University Press, 1981).

T. Kneisner, A. Padilla, and S. Polachek, "The Rate of Return to Schooling and the Business Cycle," *Journal of Human Resources* 13, no. 2 (1978): 264-77.

H. Levin, "Education and Earnings of Blacks and the *Brown* Decision," in *Have We Overcome?,* ed. M. Namorato (Jackson, Miss.: University Press of Mississippi, 1979), 79-119.

S. H. Masters, *Black-White Income Differentials* (New York: Academic Press, 1975).

D. W. Rasmussen, "A Note on the Relative Income of Nonwhite Men 1948-1964," *Quarterly Journal of Economics* 84 (February 1970): 168-72.

M. Reich, *Racial Inequality, A Political-Economic Analysis* (Princeton: Princeton University Press, 1981).

J. P. Smith and F. Welch, *Race Differences in Earnings: A Survey and New Evidence* (Santa Monica, Cal.: Rand, March 1978).

L. C. Thurow, *Poverty and Discrimination* (Washington, D.C.: Brookings, 1969).

L. Weiss and J. G. Williamson, "Black Education, Earnings, and Interregional Migration: Some New Evidence," *American Economic Review* 62 (June 1972): 372-83.

R. D. Weiss, "The Effects of Education on the Earnings of Blacks and Whites," *Review of Economics and Statistics* 52 (May 1970): 159-59.

RACIAL DIFFERENCES IN UNEMPLOYMENT: A SPATIAL PERSPECTIVE

Joe T. Darden

THE GEOGRAPHIC FRAMEWORK

Geographers have only recently become aware of the fact that spatial variation in social and economic conditions are important in understanding the state of racial justice or social well-being in a nation.

The concept of social justice is concerned with distribution and retribution of society's scarce resources and other benefits as they are allocated between different individuals and groups (Titmuss, 1962, pp. 21-35). The question of distribution is of particular importance to social well-being. The distribution of individual welfare, i.e., how many have how much (or how little), must be taken into account as well as how much there is overall (Winter et al., 1968, p. 320). To date, little attention has been given to the geography of social well-being in the United States, for geographers have been preoccupied with physical and economic conditions while most sociologists are not accustomed to thinking in spatial terms (Smith, 1973, p. xi). The contemporary social indicators movement is an important reflection of changing criteria of "relevance" with respect to the activities of social scientists and the concerns of society at large (Smith, 1973, p. xi). Yet it has attracted very little explicit attention in geographical circles, including those that emphasize social responsibility (Smith, 1973, p. xi).

Among the first geographers to view geography within the conceptual framework of social justice were David Harvey (1972) and David Smith (1973). Harvey has argued that the present spatial distribution of resources is socially unjust because the needs of the people of each territory are not met (Harvey, 1972, p. 21). Smith's (1973) book was directly concerned with geographical variations in social well-being in the United States. It was probably the first effort to align geography with the social indicators movement. More recently, Coates, Johnston, and Knox (1977) have examined the variation of social well-being on both a national and international scale. They described the spatial patterns of inequalities and attempted to explain why they occurred. They concluded that three sets of reasons are important. In the first, they argue that the division of labor has a clear spatial pattern. Since the rewards of an economic society (e.g., wealth, status, and power) are differentially distributed, with the working class generally under-privileged, this spatial division of labor produces a spatial pattern of inequalities.

The central issue of this paper is how to deal with the question of unemployment when individuals are differentiated with respect to race as well as geographic location.

It has been well documented that in economic good times and economic hard times, unemployment rates of Blacks and Hispanics in the United States have remained much higher than the rates of whites (Green, Darden, Hirt, Simmons, Tenbrunsel, Thomas, Thomas, and Thomas, 1981). Among Blacks, for example, unemployment rates have been, on the average, twice as high as those for whites since racial data on unemployment became available in 1948 (Table 1). But is racial difference in unemployment at the national level also prevalent to the same degree at the metropolitan level? In other words, are there spatial variations in racial differences in unemployment rates in large metropolitan areas? Which metropolitan areas have the least racial inequality, and which ones have the most? What is the regional distribution of unemployment patterns? Finally, why do spatial variations in racial differences in unemployment exist, i.e., are there correlates between unemployment differences and other socioeconomic and demographic variables?

It is the purpose of this paper to address these questions by assessing racial differences in unemployment rates from 1974 to 1979 in the largest metropolitan areas of the United States. Based on data availability, this study is limited to an assessment of racial differences in unemployment between Blacks and whites and Hispanics and whites.

Data and Method

Data for this paper were obtained from the U.S. Department of Labor's Current Population Surveys (CPS), sample surveys of households con-

TABLE 1
Black/White Differences in Unemployment Rates, 1948-79

| Year | Unemployment Rate | | Ratio: Black and Other Races to White |
	Black and Other Races	White	
1948	5.9	3.5	1.7
1949	8.9	5.6	1.6
1950	9.0	4.9	1.8
1951	5.3	3.1	1.7
1952	5.4	2.8	1.9
1953	4.5	2.7	1.7
1954	9.9	5.0	2.0
1955	8.7	3.9	2.2
1956	8.3	3.6	2.3
1957	7.9	3.8	2.1
1958	12.6	6.1	2.1
1959	10.7	4.8	2.2
1960	10.2	4.9	2.1
1961	12.4	6.0	2.1
1962	10.9	4.9	2.2
1963	10.8	5.0	2.2
1964	9.6	4.6	2.1
1965	8.1	4.1	2.0
1966	7.3	3.3	2.2
1967	7.4	3.4	2.2
1968	6.7	3.2	2.1
1969	6.4	3.1	2.1
1970	8.2	4.5	1.8
1971	9.9	5.4	1.8
1972	10.0	5.0	2.0

TABLE 1 (continued)

Year	Black and Other Races	White	Ratio: Black and Other Races to White
1973	8.9	4.3	2.1
1974	9.9	5.0	2.0
1975	13.9	7.8	1.8
1976	13.1	7.0	1.9
1977	13.1	6.2	2.1
1978	11.9	5.2	2.3
1979	11.3	5.1	2.2

Source: Computed by the author from data obtained from U.S. Department of Commerce. Bureau of the Census. Current Population Surveys, 1974-1979. Conducted for the Bureau of Labor Statistics. Washington, D.C., 1975-1980.

ducted monthly by the Bureau of the Census for the Bureau of Labor Statistics. The Current Population Surveys are the basis of the national unemployment rates. The Current Population Surveys provide information about the labor force activity of the entire civilian noninstitutional population 16 years of age and over in each of the metropolitan areas in this study. Each person is classified as either employed, unemployed, or not in the labor force. To be classified as unemployed, an individual must: (1) have been without a job during the survey week, (2) have made specific efforts to find employment sometime during the prior four weeks of the survey, and (3) be presently available for work. In addition, persons on layoff and those waiting to begin a new job (within 30 days), neither of whom must meet the job-seeking requirements, are also classified as unemployed. The unemployment rate represents the unemployed as a proportion of the civilian labor force, (i.e., the employed and unemployed combined).

Simple ratios were used to measure the racial differences in unemployment rates. The black unemployment rate, for example, was divided into the white unemployment rate. Thus, a ratio of 1.0 reflects no racial difference in unemployment, and the greater the deviation from 1.0 the greater the racial disparity in unemployment.

Because the data used in this study are based on samples rather than complete counts of the population, some caution is advised in its interpretation. For information about the reliability of the data, the reader should consult the following U.S. Department of Labor publications: *Geographic Profile of Employment and Unemployment* (1974, Report 452, Appendix E; 1975, Report 481, Appendix E; 1976, Report 504, Appendix C); *State Profile of Employment and Unemployment* (1977, Report 539, Appendix A); *Geographic Profile of Employment and Unemployment: States* (1978, Report 571, Appendix A); and *Geographic Profile of Employment and Unemployment* (1979).

In a geographical inquiry of this kind, the choice of the spatial scale at which to operate was an important consideration. This work uses the metropolitan area as the spatial unit instead of the central city because there is reason to believe that the former better reflects the heterogeneous nature of urban unemployment patterns.

Metropolitan areas contain human resources ranging from the most educated to the most marginally employable, and occupations ranging from managers and professionals to mass production workers requiring a narrow set of skills to the most menial jobs in the service trades (Coates, Johnston, & Knox, 1977: 136). These differences are compounded by, as well as related to, ethnic, religious, and racial characteristics. The unequal distribution of the employed and unemployed is one result of this plethora of conflicting pressures and interlocking attributes of metropolitan life (Coates, Johnston, & Knox, 1977, p. 136).

The central cities of metropolitan areas are becoming increasingly homogeneous in marked contrast to the central cities of the past. Hence, the metropolitan area has become the "functional and structural equivalent of the older central city" (Rich, 1979, p. 48). The metropolitan area today functions much as local areas have functioned traditionally as regards to the spatial distribution of races and classes, and the differential access to jobs and other opportunities. To the extent that metropolitan populations are interdependent rather than independent by dint of municipal boundaries, it is appropriate to expand the concern for equity issues to the metropolitan area (Williams, 1971; Harvey, 1973). Neiman (1975, p. 37) argues that "the latent function of the metropolis, as an aggregate, macro-level entity, is to maintain and increase, through structure and policy, the unequal access of individuals to 'the good life,' " through impediments to movement for one set of individuals and various subsidies for the pursuit of a locational strategy by other individuals (see Darden, 1980).

Black and White Unemployment Differences in Selected Metropolitan Areas, 1974-79

The reader is advised that the data on black unemployment as provided by the Bureau of Labor Statistics and presented here also include other non-whites (i.e., American Indians, Alaskan natives, Asian and Pacific islanders). Although the inclusion of these additional groups may have some effect on the unemployment statistics, the effect is probably very minor since Blacks constitute the overwhelming majority of non-whites.

Whereas, the national unemployment rate of black workers was double that of white workers during the study period, 1974-1979, there was wide variation in the size of the gap between the unemployment rates of these groups among the nation's largest Standard Metropolitan Statistical Areas (SMSAs). Data on black unemployment was available for 27 of the largest metropolitan areas during 1974-1979. When compared to the white rate of unemployment, the racial disparities are clear cut and persistent. Because most studies of racial disparities in unemployment have focused only on the national scale, the intensity, differences, and *internal* spatial variation in the pattern of unemployment have not been clearly revealed. Racial inequality, as other phenomena, tends to vary spatially. As indicated in Table 2, racial disparities in unemployment are worse than the national average in 15 of the 24 metropolitan areas surveyed, or 63 percent. The most severe inequality in the workforce has occurred in Kansas City where the mean black unemployment rate from 1974 to 1979 was four times the white rate. Milwaukee and Nassau had black rates that were three times the white rates. Such severe racial inequality is not revealed in national unemployment figures where the gap was only 2:1, or a black rate twice the white rate (Table 2). All but two of the metropolitan areas where the unemployment gap was less than the national average are located in the South and West, areas commonly referred to as the Sunbelt.

Black/white differences in unemployment vary by regions. The greatest difference exists in metropolitan areas of the North-Central region (2.9) and the least difference exists in metropolitan areas in the West (1.8) (See Table 2). In fact, only in metropolitan areas of the West has the black unemployment rate been *less* than twice the white unemployment rate from 1974 to 1979. In general, the black/white difference in unemploy-

TABLE 2
Rank Order of Largest Metropolitan Areas by Mean Black/White
Unemployment Gap, 1974-79

Rank	Area	Mean Unemployment Gap
1	Kansas City	4.0
2	Milwaukee	3.7
3	Nassau	3.2
4	Philadelphia	2.8
4	St. Louis	2.8
5	Baltimore	2.7
5	Chicago	2.7
6	Cincinnati	2.6
6	Houston	2.6
7	Atlanta	2.5
7	Indianapolis	2.5
8	Pittsburgh	2.4
8	Washington, D.C.	2.4
9	Detroit	2.3
9	Cleveland	2.3
		U.S. Average Gap 2.1
10	Dallas	2.1
10	Newark	2.1
10	Seattle	2.1
11	Miami	1.9
12	San Francisco	1.8
13	Los Angeles	1.7
14	Boston	1.4
14	New York	1.4
14	San Diego	1.4
	Mean	2.4

Source: Computed by the author from data obtained from U.S. Department of Commerce. Bureau of the Census. *Current Population Surveys, 1974-1979.* Conducted for the Bureau of Labor Statistics. Washington, D.C., 1975-1980.

TABLE 3
Mean Black/White Unemployment Gap by Regions in Metropolitan Areas

Metropolitan Area	Mean Black/White Difference
	Gap 1974-79
	North Central Region
Kansas City	4.0
Milwaukee	3.7
St. Louis	2.8
Chicago	2.7
Cincinnati	2.6
Indianapolis	2.5
Cleveland	2.3
Detroit	2.3
Regional Mean	2.9
	Northeast Region
Nassau	3.2
Philadelphia	2.8
Pittsburgh	2.4
Newark	2.1
Boston	1.4
New York	1.4
Regional Mean	2.2

ment is greater in the large metropolitan areas (2.4) than for all areas in the United States (2.1).

Hispanic and White Unemployment Differences in Selected Metropolitan Areas

Since unemployment rates for Hispanic workers in metropolitan areas were not available prior to 1976, the study period is limited to 1976-1979 and to the six Standard Metropolitan Statistical Areas (SMSAs) for which Hispanic data were distinguishable. These six areas include Chicago, Houston, Los Angeles, Miami, New York, and San Francisco. The ratio of Hispanic to white unemployment rates was much smaller than the ratio

TABLE 3 (continued)

Metropolitan Area	Mean Black/White Difference
	Gap 1974-79
The South	
Baltimore	2.7
Houston	2.6
Atlanta	2.5
Washington, D.C.	2.4
Dallas	2.1
Miami	1.9
Regional Mean	2.4
The West	
Seattle	2.1
San Francisco	1.8
Los Angeles	1.7
San Diego	1.4
Regional Mean	1.8

Source: Computed by the author from data obtained from U.S. Department of Commerce. Bureau of the Census. Current Population Surveys, 1974-1979. Conducted for the Bureau of Labor Statistics. Washington, D.C., 1975-1980.

of Blacks to whites each year from 1976 to 1979 in the five metropolitan areas studied. In no metropolitan area was the ratio of the unemployment rate for Hispanic workers twice that of white workers. Contrary to the ratios between Blacks and whites, the ratios between Hispanics and whites were lower in large metropolitan areas (1.4) than in the nation as a whole (1.7) from 1976 to 1979. Similar to the racial difference pattern between Blacks and whites, the unemployment gap was large between Hispanics and whites in the metropolitan areas of the North-Central and Northeast regions (Chicago and New York) and small in the metropolitan areas in the South and West (Houston, Miami, San Francisco, and Los Angeles) (See Table 3.)

Factors in the Persistent Unemployment Gap
Between Blacks and Whites

It is apparent from the data that much of the metropolitan unemployment problem consists primarily of black and, to a lesser extent, Hispanic unemployment.

Past research indicates that several factors may account for the persistent black/white unemployment gap. Racial discrimination in employment is a major factor, despite antidiscrimination policies. Most black workers have been disproportionally concentrated in semiskilled, low-wage jobs, with few opportunities for upward mobility where the unemployment rate is traditionally lower (Darden, 1974). Black job holders continue to be underrepresented in skilled blue-collar jobs (U.S. Congress, 1978, p. 11). To some extent, the current pattern of inequality reflects the accumulated product of past discrimination rather than current actions, but progress against systematic forms of discrimination has been slow and uneven across industries. Racial discrimination has also limited the spatial mobility of Blacks, restricting Blacks to the central cities where fewer jobs exist. Thus, almost 60% of the black unemployed compared to only 27% of the unemployed whites live in central cities (U.S. Congress, 1978, p. 10). Because Blacks have been disproportionally employed in semiskilled occupations and manufacturing industries in the older central cities of the North and East, they have been the most affected by plant closings in these areas. Massive layoffs, especially of low-seniority workers, which includes a substantial number of Blacks, have occurred in manufacturing industries such as steel and auto. In 1979, manufacturing accounted for only 20.7 million of 86.7 million nonagricultural wage and salary jobs in the United States (Sternlieb and Hughes, 1980, p. 51). Much of the manufacturing that was once done in the cities of the North and East has moved to the South and West and to foreign countries. Thus, the United States as a whole is losing manufacturing jobs. Much of the garment manufacturing once done in New York City, for example, is now done in places such as Taiwan. Furthermore, the postindustrial service economy has failed to generate anywhere near the number of jobs that have been lost because of departed manufacturing (Sternlieb and Hughes, 1980, p. 51). Significant numbers of the few jobs remaining in the central cities are held by white suburbanites. This geographic mismatch has added to the already high black unemployment rate.

Past research suggests that racial differences in unemployment are associated with racial differences in the occupational structure. Because blacks, whites, and Hispanic workers are unevenly distributed within the occupational structure of metropolitan areas, and unemployment rates vary by occupation, these workers experience differential unemployment rates. Although some researchers have discussed this relationship conceptually, few have demonstrated the relationship empirically. In the section that follows, it is shown that the black/white unemployment ratios of metropolitan areas are correlated with the unemployment rates of occupations. Such correlations explain the variation in unemployment ratios by metropolitan area and region.

CORRELATES OF RACIAL DIFFERENCES IN UNEMPLOYMENT WITH UNEMPLOYMENT RATES BY OCCUPATION

Based on prior research, two hypotheses can be stated. Hypothesis 1: There is an inverse correlation between black/white unemployment ratios and rates of unemployment of (a) white-collar workers and (b) skilled blue-collar workers in metropolitan areas. Hypothesis 2: There is a positive correlation between black/white unemployment ratios and rates of unemployment of (a) semiskilled blue-collar workers and (b) unskilled workers in metropolitan areas. Hypothesis 1 leads us to expect low ratios of black-to-white unemployment rates in the West and high ratios in the North-Central region. Hypothesis 2 leads us to expect the same pattern.

Due to limited available data for comparative purposes, this analysis is restricted to the year 1978 and to black and white workers in the 24 metropolitan areas shown in Table 1. As indicated in Table 4, there is a significant inverse correlation between black/white unemployment ratios and all white-collar workers except sales workers. The strongest correlation (-.61) exists between black/white unemployment ratios and unemployment rates of professional, technical, and kindred workers. A significant inverse correlation (-.38) also exists between black/white unemployment ratios and unemployment rates of skilled blue-collar workers. Thus, Hypotheses 1 is supported.

Hypothesis 2, on the other hand, is not supported. No significant positive correlation exists between black/white unemployment ratios and rates of unemployment of semiskilled blue-collar workers and unskilled workers.

TABLE 4
Mean Hispanic/White Differences in Unemployment Rates, 1976-79,
in Selected Metropolitan Areas

Area	1976	1977	1978	1979	Mean Ratio 1976-1979
United States	1.7	1.6	1.8	1.6	1.7
Chicago	1.6	1.5	1.9	1.9	1.7
Houston*	1.0	1.3	0.9	1.1	1.1
Los Angeles	1.4	1.3	1.4	1.4	1.4
Miami	1.3	1.1	1.2	1.1	1.2
New York*	1.3	1.3	1.5	1.7	1.5
San Francisco	1.4	1.2	1.6	1.0	1.3
Mean	1.3	1.3	1.4	1.4	1.4

*These data for the Hispanic population·are based on the 1970

geographic boundary definition for the SMSA. Therefore, they are

not strictly comparable with data for the other areas.

Source: Computed by the author from data obtained from U.S. Department

of Commerce. Bureau of the Census. Current Population Surveys,

1974-1979. Conducted for the Bureau of Labor Statistics.

Washington, D.C., 1975-1980.

CONCLUSIONS

It has been demonstrated that racial differences in unemployment in the
nation's largest metropolitan areas are widespread. The differences tend
to vary, however, by region with the greatest difference occurring in the
metropolitan areas of the North-Central region and the least difference
occurring in the metropolitan areas in the West.

The reasons for such variation in unemployment differences were examined. The results revealed that metropolitan areas with the highest unemployment rates among professional, technical and kindred workers,
managers and administrators, clerical workers, and craft and kindred
workers, combined with the lowest rates of unemployment among service

workers, tend to have the lowest black/white unemployment ratios. These areas were more prevalent in the West in 1978. On the other hand, those metropolitan areas with the lowest unemployment rates of professional, technical, and· kindred workers, managers and administrators, clerical workers, and craft and kindred workers, combined with the highest rates of unemployment among service workers, tend to have the highest black/white unemployment ratios. These areas were more prevalent in the North-Central region in 1978.

The significance of these findings suggests that any study of racial differences in unemployment must examine unemployment using disaggregated data. Furthermore, any policy designed to reduce the gap between black and white unemployment rates in metropolitan areas must address the problem of variations in unemployment rates by occupational category.

REFERENCES

Coates, B.E., R.J. Johnston, and P.L. Knox, *Geography and Inequality.* Oxford: Oxford University Press, 1977.

Darden, Joe T., "Lending Practices and Policies Affecting the American Metropolitan System" in *The American Metropolitan System: Present and Future.* Edited by Stanley D. Brunn and James O. Wheeler. New York: V.H. Winston and Sons, 1980, 93-110.

Green, Robert L., Joe T. Darden, Jill Hirt, Cassandra Simmons, Thomas Tenbrunsel, Frances S. Thomas, June M. Thomas, and Richard W. Thomas, *Discrimination and the Welfare of Urban Minorities.* Springfield, Illinois: Charles Thomas, 1981.

Harvey, David, *Social Justice and the City.* Baltimore: Johns Hopkins University Press, 1973.

Harvey, David, "Social Justice in Spatial Systems" in R. Peet, ed., *Geographical Perspectives on American Poverty,* Antipode Monographs in Social Geography no. 1. Worchester, Mass., 1972, 87-106.

Neiman, M., *Metropology.* Beverly Hills: Sage, 1975.

Rich, Richard, "Neglected Issues in the Study of Urban Service Distributions: A Research Agenda," in Urban Studies 16, 1979, 143-156.

Smith, David, *The Geography of Social Well-Being in the United States.* New York: McGraw Hill, 1973.

Sternlieb, George, and James Hughes, "The Changing Demography of the Central City" in *Scientific American,* August 1980, 48-53.

Titmuss, R., *Income Distribution and Social Change.* London: Allen and Univen, 1962.

U.S. Congress, Joint Economic Committee, "Structural Unemployment and Urban Policy." Hearing Before the Subcommittee on Economic Growth and Stabilization of the Joint Economic Committee, 95th Congress, 2nd Session, March 1978. Washington, D.C.: U.S. Government Printing Office.

Williams, O.P., *Metropolitan Political Analysis.* New York: The Free Press, 1971.

Winter, J.A., et al., eds., *Vital Problems for American Society: Meanings and Means.* New York: Random House, 1968.

ABOUT THE AUTHORS

Nancy S. Barrett, Ph.D., is professor of economics at American University and a former deputy assistant secretary with the U.S. Department of Labor.

Barry Bluestone, Ph.D., is professor of economics and director of the Social Welfare Research Institute at Boston College.

Joe T. Darden, Ph.D., is professor of geography and urban affairs at Michigan State University.

Donald J. Harris, Ph.D., is professor of economics at Stanford University.

Everson Hill, Ph.D., is deputy assistant secretary for research and technical support in the Office of Policy at the U.S. Department of Labor, and former head of the Money and Banking Section of the Economics Division at the Congressional Research Service.

Glenn C. Loury, Ph.D., is professor of economics and Afro-American studies at Harvard University.

David H. Swinton, Ph.D., is director of the Southern Center for Studies in Public Policy at Clark College and the 1983 president of the National Economic Association.